DONOGHUE'S INVESTMENT TIPS FOR RETIREMENT SAVINGS

By the same author

William E. Donoghue's Complete Money Market Guide

William E. Donoghue's No-Load Mutual Fund Guide

William E. Donoghue's Guide to Finding Money to Invest

William E. Donoghue's Lifetime Financial Planner

William E. Donoghue

Donoghue's Investment Tips for Retirement Savings

REVISED EDITION

PERENNIAL LIBRARY

HARPER & ROW, PUBLISHERS, New York
Cambridge, Philadelphia, San Francisco, Washington
London, Mexico City, São Paulo, Singapore, Sydney

For the American worker

First PERENNIAL LIBRARY edition published 1987.

Designer: Sidney Feinberg
Copyeditor: Ann Finlayson
Indexer: Auralie Logan

ISBN: 0-06-096148-1
LIBRARY OF CONGRESS CATALOG CARD NUMBER: 86-45761
87 88 89 90 91 MPC 10 9 8 7 6 5 4 3 2 1

Contents

Acknowledgments

The long road to tax reform is littered with drafts of this book. If you've ever tried to "shoot the bobbing bear" at a carnival, you'll appreciate what we went through trying to write this book as Congress debated the new tax bill. At times, the shape of the new law changed hourly. (When the tax reformers finally agreed on the bill's provisions, we were jubilant, to say the least.)

The excellent and, literally, tireless staff of professionals who helped me craft this work deserve special thanks.

Mary C. Driscoll, vice president of editorial at The Donoghue Organization, must be commended for her project leadership and editing acumen. Dana Shilling, a talented lawyer and financial writer (who is also my collaborator on *William E. Donoghue's Lifetime Financial Planner,* published recently by Harper & Row), lent her sharp analytical skills and dauntless energy to this endeavor. Cynthia C. Andrade, CFA, our manager of research, wrote some of the more complex chapters. Connie Bugbee, editor of *Donoghue's Money Fund Report,* and Lisa Harrison, editor of *Donoghue's Moneyletter,* helped with the research and editing. Gail Scho, our art director, made the production of this book possible. Leslie McDonnell, our editorial assistant, proved invaluable.

Special thanks also goes to Peter Reilly, CPA with Joseph Cohan & Associates, in Worcester, Mass., who helped us analyze the new tax code.

Finally, I want to thank our good friends at Harper & Row: Ed Burlingame, publisher, and Sallie Coolidge, editor.

Preface:
Take Charge of Your Retirement
Savings Plan

As W. C. Fields once said, "There comes a time in the affairs of man when you must take the bull by the tail and face the situation." Now is the time for you to take responsibility for your retirement security.

The specter of an ailing Social Security system, continued economic uncertainty and the fact that the U.S. work force as a whole is aging have many working Americans worried about financial survival in the years after retirement. Being elderly and broke is not a pretty picture. But your future security—and your family's future security—need not be jeopardized. No matter how old you are today, you can act now, before it's too late.

Use the Tools Congress Gave You

Although the Tax Reform Act of 1986 limited the appeal of certain retirement plans, American workers still have a powerful arsenal of retirement planning vehicles at their disposal. In the pages that follow, you'll learn which ones represent the best deals today and how you can put them to work for you.

It's useful to note that during the five years preceding adoption of the new law, Congress had been extremely generous in doling out tax breaks to folks who wanted to build healthy retirement nest eggs. The sense among politicians at that time was that Americans did not feel comfortable relying solely on Social Security and company pensions to take care of them after retirement. Congress therefore provided compelling tax incentives so people would build their own financial reserves to augment traditional sources of retirement income.

However, when it came time to write the new tax reform law, Congress realized it had gone overboard in the past. Data showed that many Americans were not in fact using IRAs and 401(k) plans to save for retirement but, rather, were using them as tax-advantaged savings accounts—to fund preretirement activities such as home rehabilitation, vacationing, and planning for college tuitions. Congress became convinced that it had been giving away the store, so to speak. The new tax law was thus used to tighten up perceived abuses of tax-advantaged retirement investing. (What tipped the scales was that Congress knew it could pay for the lowering of the tax rates by restricting retirement plans.)

Political trends notwithstanding, the fact remains that Americans should not depend complacently on Social Security and pensions. Throughout this book, we urge you to use the tools Congress gave you, even if some, most notably IRAs, are not as fantastic as they once were. If you are willing to put a little elbow grease into the planning process—the earlier the better!—you can build a comfortable, indeed, financially secure retirement.

Remember, the importance of retirement investing was not diminished by tax reform. To the contrary. Because some vehicles, such as IRAs, lost some of their wealth-building power, it's all the more critical that you learn how to get the most out of the retirement plans you are allowed to use today. You'll need to manage, for maximum efficiency, your family's basket of retirement products, including tax-deferred annuities, 401(k) plans, Keoghs, 403(b) and 403(b)(7) plans, and, yes, IRAs. Despite the new tax law, millions of Americans are still entitled to contribute tax-deductible annual contributions to IRAs. Even if you're not allowed to deduct your IRA contributions, as we'll demonstrate in Chapter 2, you can still invest in an IRA and have your earnings compound tax-free until you begin withdrawals.

"Is it really worth it," you ask, "to keep putting money into an IRA when the tax deduction is wiped out or reduced?" Assuredly, yes!

Consider this. Say you've got $2,000 to invest for retirement each year. You must now decide whether to put it in an IRA—where earnings compound tax-free until withdrawal—or put it in some other investment that is fully taxable. If you put that $2,000 in an IRA, and if you earn 10 percent each year for 25 years, and if you're in the 28% tax bracket, your IRA investment will be worth $113,253 more than a comparable taxable investment. The power of tax-deferred savings growth cannot be ignored. What's more, by funding your IRA each year, you are essentially putting yourself on a forced savings program. (The tax penalty for early withdrawal will discourage you from tapping your retirement money to pay for truly nonessential purchases.) When it comes time to retire, you'll pat yourself on the back for making a smart financial decision.

Jargon Busting

Without question, the jargon alone is dizzying (and the thought of pulling it all together downright intimidating). For some people, the legal mumbo jumbo is too much, and they simply give up—thereby casting their fates to the wind. That's why we decided to write this book: to help you get a handle on the basic terms and techniques of retirement investing. We're convinced that if you'll commit a little quiet reading time, you'll begin to see that you can take matters into your own hands and assure your retirement comfort. You'll also see that a few sound, easy-to-use investment strategies can make your golden years the best ever.

Why aren't retirement plans clearly explained by the organizations providing them? A few basic clues: (1) the low $2,000 annual contribution limits on IRAs offer investment salespeople little profit incentive to give you personalized advice; (2) laws governing certain employer plans actually discourage the employer from giving you in-depth investment coaching, and; (3) the IRS has been very slow in clarifying the details of many attractive plans—consequently, many smaller financial service firms wait to make sure they do "the right thing." As a result, they do nothing.

Help Has Arrived

In the pages that follow, you'll find the help you need to make practical decisions about your family's retirement savings program. In addition to learning exactly how various retirement plans work, you'll learn how to incorporate them into an overall management strategy that's right for you. You'll benefit from:

- the ability to separate sales hype from valid product offerings.
- down-to-earth tips on investment decision making.
- insight into how the tools already at your disposal can be used to maximize your retirement income and cut your current federal tax bill at the same time.
- details on tax-deferred compounding and the fantastic earnings growth it provides.
- advice on how to cope with pension plan terminations or changes.
- advice on managing your assets and taxes once you're retired.
- a sobering look at how medical bills can devastate your retirement savings and advice on avoiding Medicare pitfalls.

Advice for Readers of All Ages

The biggest mistake you can make is to assume that any book about retirement planning is for "older people." The fact is that no one can guarantee our nation's continued economic prosperity—and no one can say whether or not the federal government will be able to maintain its subsidy of many social service programs we now take for granted. The real question you must ask yourself is: Do I really want to depend on the government to take care of me when I'm 75?

Just stop for a moment and think about the basic concept of supply and demand. In the not-too-distant future, there may actually be a shortage of skilled workers in America. Who will fund Social Security —and who will pay taxes—in the year 2000? The only smart way to cope with these issues is to begin taking an active role in securing your own retirement nest egg. Getting a head start now means doing yourself—and your family—a giant favor.

Furthermore, wise retirement planning means much more than simply stashing money away. For instance, you may want to utilize your retirement assets in different ways during different stages of your life. Younger readers in their twenties or thirties will perhaps want to know how to tap into their retirement savings temporarily—just after getting married, when building or buying a first home or when it's time to pay for graduate school.

Middle-aged readers in their forties and fifties may need help financing a child's college tuition and still need to maximize their savings for retirement.

Folks rapidly approaching retirement must know how to restructure their investment goals to preserve their hard-earned capital. They also need practical strategies for withdrawing money from various retirement plans while preserving certain tax advantages.

Everyone will want to gain a basic understanding of financial markets so that, no matter what life brings, they can guide their investments down a rational course and avoid investment pitfalls.

It's up to You

As we shaped this book, our unwavering goal was to help you gain the confidence you need to select useful retirement products, invest wisely, and make sound decisions about your financial security. There is a versatile set of planning tools available today. What follows is practical advice for putting those tools to work. After that, it's up to you.

1 The Lowdown on Retirement: What to Expect

Retirement can be a wonderful time in your life, or it can be a living hell that destroys family harmony. While you can't stop the clock, you can take steps to assure your retirement comfort. The first, and most important, step is determining the financial resources you'll need later on in life.

In the chapters that follow, we'll explain how you can use a variety of savings programs and investment strategies to build your nest egg. We'll also counsel you on some of the financial choices you face. First, however, we'll look at how your financial picture will change once you've retired.

An old saying is apropos: If you want to have a successful journey, you have to know exactly where you're headed. When it comes to retirement planning, you'll need to project the retirement income that would be available to you given your current financial status. If you realize that it won't meet your needs comfortably, you can take action now to boost your postretirement prosperity.

Spring Planting, Fall Harvest

During most of your working life, any financial planning you do is probably focused on salary, benefits, and investment earnings—and finding ways to stretch these funds to meet your family's short-term and long-term needs. However, your working life is also the time for planning, planting, and tending your retirement garden.

Retirement is the time to harvest. You finally leave your regular job

—either exiting the job world entirely or changing to another kind of paid work or to volunteer work. You start depending on different sources of income on which to live. Instead of salary and bonuses, you now rely on pension payments, Social Security benefits, funds withdrawn from IRA, Keogh, and other retirement savings accounts, and, of course, the cash flow from your investments.

You'll probably find that your expenses decrease during retirement. The kid's college tuition bills no longer cause major headaches—if you're lucky, neither do the kids. They may still need your help once in a while, but they've gone off on their own. The worst is past.

What's more, the mortgage is paid off and no longer puts a drain on your paycheck. The "dress for success" wardrobe has been replaced with well-worn fishing and golf clothes instead of expensive suits. All in all, your income stretches a bit further. (Of course, large medical bills are inevitable for many retirees. We'll show you how to cope with medical costs in Chapter 10.)

Realistic Plans

It's fun to have daydreams about travel and motorboats, but it's much more helpful to get an accurate idea of what your retirement income will be. Then, if you have the money to travel, buy the boat you've always wanted, or redecorate your house, you can enjoy these pleasures with an easy mind.

The first step in making a postretirement budget is to estimate the way your expenses will change. If you're an apartment dweller, the city in which you live may give you some protection against rent increases and eviction after you reach age 65. Call City Hall and check out your rights.

If you're a homeowner, chances are pretty good that the mortgage will be paid off by the time you retire; and you may also qualify for property tax relief as a senior citizen. Check with your accountant.

You won't have any more work-related expenses, but your leisure and entertainment costs will probably increase. Medical bills are impossible to budget (unless you belong to a Health Maintenance Organization that covers all medical and hospitalization costs), but you'll need a reserve of some kind for them. Also note that unless you turn down Medicare Part B, the monthly premium (currently $17.90) will be deducted from your Social Security check. (See Chapter 10 for details on Medicare.)

What About the House?

If you do own your home, you might want to sell it and move either to a smaller house, condo or apartment in your area, or move to a warmer climate. One good reason for doing this is the tax break for senior citizens: you can make a profit of up to $125,000 on the sale of your home without having to pay any tax on the profit. (These rules are a little different if you used part of the home as a business, or if you lived in a multi-family house and rented out part of it.)

The profit on your home can be a very useful retirement nest egg. However, there's a reason for being cautious about this strategy: If you or your spouse ever needs to qualify for Medicaid, funds in a bank account or investment are likely to disqualify you. Home ownership will not.

If you don't want to move, you have several interesting choices today: equity access loans and reverse mortgages. Using an equity access loan, you can borrow an amount that is based on the equity in your house. You are free, then, to do what you wish with the proceeds (within certain legal constraints).

Using a reverse mortgage to raise cash is an innovative strategy that allows you to sell your home to a broker who then lets you live in your home and pays you a fixed amount each month. When you die, the broker will settle with your estate for the remaining value of your home equity.

The Tax Code of 1986 (which we'll refer to as TC '86 in the balance of this book) changed the rules about deductibility of consumer interest in a way that makes equity access loans unusually attractive. By 1991, you will no longer be able to deduct all the interest expenses you incur when you take out a consumer loan or run up your credit cards. (These deductions are phased out beginning in 1987.) However, TC '86 lets you deduct interest expenses incurred when you borrow on the equity in your first or second home. And you can use these home equity loans to finance big ticket items such as college tuitions. (We urge you *not* to use your home equity as collateral for vacations, motorboats, and the like. After all, you are putting your home on the line.)

Both programs allow you to access the equity value in your home and use it to generate cash flow. The best part is that you don't have to move out. If you're interested in how these programs might benefit you or a family member, ask your bank for details—but be sure to check out any deal with a lawyer before you sign on the dotted line.

Retirement Income

Most retirees can count on having at least some Social Security benefits—for many, these benefits are the major source of post-retirement income. (More about Social Security in Chapter 2.)

Social Security

The amount of Social Security benefits depends on whether you retire (1) at the normal retirement age, which is currently 65—the normal retirement age will be increased gradually starting in the year 2000, (2) early—in which case your benefits will be reduced, or (3) after the normal retirement age—in which case your benefits will be increased because you'll be drawing them for a shorter time.

The Social Security benefit also depends on your Primary Insurance Amount (PIA), which is based on the way your average annual income compares to the maximum amount on which Social Security taxes can be collected. Benefits are available for retired workers and their dependents (spouse, widow, ex-spouse, widowed ex-spouse, surviving children, surviving parents, etc.). A married woman who worked outside her home can collect benefits as the spouse of a retired worker, or as a retired worker, but not both.

Company Pension

Many retirees are also entitled to a pension from their former employers. (See Chapters 3 and 9.) There are two major kinds of pension plans: defined benefit and defined contribution. In a defined benefit plan, the employer sets a level of retirement benefits (for instance, a monthly pension of 2% of the average income the employee earned in his or her three highest-paid years). Then, after consulting financial advisers and actuaries (actuaries are a particular kind of statistician who advise insurance firms and pension plans), the employer makes contributions for the employee's benefit to the pension plan each year. The contributions are designed to fund the benefit amount.

In a defined contribution plan, the employer sets a level of contribution for each employee (let's say 2% of the employee's annual salary). This amount is contributed to a special pension account for the employee. The employee's pension will be based on the total amount in the account, including any investment earnings, when the employee retires.

Integration with Social Security

Some pension plans are "integrated." In an integrated plan, the employer reduces the benefit (if it's a defined benefit plan) to compensate for Social Security benefits, or reduces the contribution (if it's a defined contribution plan) to compensate for the Social Security taxes the employer pays on the employee's wages. The effect is to reduce the amount of pension the employee receives from the employer.

Your employer is required to give you an annual statement of the funds in your account (or contributions made to fund a defined benefit). You can discuss this statement with your union representative, or the company's pension and benefits or employee relations staff, and find out approximately what your pension will be if you take your pension in the form of an annuity.

Taking Your "Lumps" or Waiting

Most plans are written so that you have a choice when you retire. You can either take your pension benefits in a lump sum or in the form of an annuity. (See Chapters 3 and 9 for a discussion of the financial and tax consequences of your choice.)

If you go the annuity route, you can also choose between (1) a regular annuity (payments are usually made to you every month), (2) a lifetime annuity (either with payments stopping at your death, or continuing over the lifetime of your spouse or another beneficiary you designate), and (3) an annuity lasting for a certain number of years (the number of years can't be longer than your life expectancy or the joint life expectancies of you and your beneficiary).

IRA and Keogh Plans

If you have an IRA and/or Keogh account, you have a lot of flexibility. You can take all the money out of your account once you reach age $59\frac{1}{2}$; you can reduce the account by removing chunks of money as you need them; or you can set up a regular system of annuity payments. (See Chapters 2 and 6 for more financial and tax information.)

People who have put energy into planning their lifelong investment strategies will find that, when they retire, their investments represent a major source of income. If you've gained confidence as an investor over the years, you'll know how to balance investment risks and rewards so that your precious nest egg continues to grow safely.

You may decide that you don't need to make major changes in your portfolio strategies just because you're retired. However, you will have to deal with a few new planning twists. You'll be on-guard because

- There are tax penalties if you start to withdraw retirement income too early, if you wait too long to start payouts, or if you take too large a payout. (Don't panic about the last one—that means a lump sum well over half a million dollars, or annual payouts well over a hundred thousand a year.)

- If you escape the penalties, the general rule is that you pay income taxes on all amounts you take out of your pension, for the year in which the money is received. However, you may qualify for five-year or ten-year averaging to reduce the tax bite on lump sum distributions. (See Chapter 9.)
- The usual tradeoff is that you choose between larger payments (say, you choose your retirement benefits in the form of an annuity for ten years) and payments for a longer time (say, an annuity stretching over your life and that of your youngest child).

Taxes and Retirement

The good news—something rare in any discussion of taxes—is that people who are over 65 are entitled to use a larger standard deduction than younger taxpayers. They may also be entitled to a special tax credit, figured out on Schedule R of the Form 1040. The IRS has two free pamphlets that you may want to read: "Tax Benefits for Older Americans" (#554) and "Credit for the Elderly and the Permanently and Totally Disabled" (#524). Read the instructions for your state income tax form carefully—many states have similar provisions for senior citizens.

Taxes on Your Social Security Check

Approximately 8–10% of Social Security beneficiaries will have to pay income taxes on part of their Social Security checks. It depends on their total income, and the source of that income. If you fall into this group, you have a lot of figuring to do.

First, you'll have to find your Adjusted Gross Income (that's the amount on the last line of the first page of the Form 1040, repeated on the first line of the second page). Next, you modify this amount by certain tax advantages you've received.

Now, add this Modified Adjusted Gross Income to one-half of the

Social Security benefits you and your spouse received, if you file a joint return, or to half of *your* Social Security benefits, if you're single or filing a separate return. The next step is to subtract the base amount. The base amount is $32,000 for a joint return; $25,000 for a single person or a married person separated from his or her spouse; and, $0 for a married person filing a separate return.

Still with us? You must include the result in your taxable income. That is, you must pay taxes on the amount by which the Modified Adjusted Gross Income plus half the Social Security benefits exceeds the base amount. However, if this amount is larger than half your Social Security benefits, you can simply pay taxes on half the Social Security benefits.

If you collect a pension from your employer in the form of an annuity, your employer will withhold federal income taxes (and, in some states, state income taxes) unless you ask for an exemption.

If you have a lot of investment income, or if you are receiving income from an IRA or Keogh, there's a very good chance that you'll have to pay estimated federal income taxes every quarter. Check with an accountant, tax preparer, or financial planner for details.

Key Concepts

The first step in planning for retirement is to estimate the ways in which your expenses will change. Next, you've got to determine the retirement income you can expect—from Social Security benefits, plus amounts from your employer-provided pension, IRA, and Keogh, plus the yield from your savings and investments. When you make financial decisions, you must consider the way they'll affect your tax picture—what really counts is the amount you have left after taxes.

The more time you have before retirement, the more time you have to tailor your budget and retirement income to your projected needs. Knowing where you are going will help you get there safely and surely.

2 The Retirement Tools We All Can Use

In this chapter, we'll examine the retirement resources available to all working Americans. We'll see that an old favorite, Social Security, has lost its pristine image—in fact, there's much debate these days about the fundamental soundness of the system. A close look at Social Security mechanics shows you how to apply for benefits and how much you can expect when you retire. We'll also take an in-depth look at IRAs and annuities, how they operate and ways to make them work for you.

Social Security: Legacy of the Industrial Age

From the late 1940s to the early 1970s, hard working Americans understood that, barring major disasters, they could retire with reasonable financial security. Company pensions had become an inalienable right for union and nonunion workers alike. The Social Security System anticipated a steady stream of revenues as the baby-boom generation went to work; and, the economy had been booming since World War II. Only the truly fastidious were obsessed with private savings for retirement.

But things began to fall apart in the 1970s when the economy was hit with unprecedented levels of inflation. Our nation's lawmakers felt compelled to authorize higher Social Security benefits as rising inflation threatened the standard of living of retired Americans. Sure enough, by the mid-1970s, the Social Security System began to sprout actuarial cracks. The American dream of a hassle-free retirement was in danger.

By the late 1970s, Congress began work on legislative reforms that encouraged private savings—the idea was to wean workers off total dependency on Social Security and traditional corporate pensions. (Inflation had also taken its toll on corporate retirement benefits.) The result: IRAs, 401(k) plans, liberalized Keoghs and so on.

Despite this evolution, Social Security still represents a major source of projected retirement income for many people. That's unfortunate. Many observers contend that Social Security benefits in the year 2000 will pale by today's standards. The fact is that although Social Security to date has been a sacred cow for politicians, there's no guarantee that it will forever avoid slaughter.

In contrast, actuaries and employee benefits experts argue that the Social Security System is sound, thanks to reforms made several years ago. Will the Social Security System indeed fail to live up to its mandate? The answer is: No one can predict with absolute certainty that the system will be rock solid by the time baby-boomers begin to retire. However, it is fair to predict that younger workers today will, more likely than not, pay more money into Social Security than they'll ever see after retirement. The question you must ask yourself is whether you really want to depend on Congressional whims to safeguard your retirement security.

The Most Expensive Insurance

During 1985, the Social Security Administration disbursed an estimated total of $189.3 billion in benefits payments, primarily to retired persons and their survivors—a total of 36.8 million Americans.

Statistics show that 51% of all American workers pay more in Social Security taxes than they do in federal income taxes. Since you are paying so much in, doesn't it make sense to check on whether your Social Security records are at least correct? First, check that the Social Security Administration has your correct name and Social Security number. Next, you request a written statement from the

Administration that will detail for you the earnings reported by your employer(s).

Since Social Security benefits are based on what you have earned, it is in your best interest to make sure these records are correct. Because the statements will detail earnings for the past three years and lump together all previous earnings, it is a good idea to submit a "Request for Statement of Earnings" every three years. You can get a copy from your local Social Security office—just stop in and ask for one, or write or call and have one sent to you. (A copy of the form is shown in Appendix C.) When you receive the response, compare it to the earnings you reported on your past income tax returns. Should you find a discrepancy, follow the instructions provided by Social Security on the form.

It should go without saying that if you change your name while employed, you should notify Social Security immediately, to ensure proper credit of your earnings. There is no charge for this service.

It Takes 10 Years to Join the Club

Most of us will need to have worked for 10 years before we can collect retirement benefits from Social Security. The following table indicates how much work credit is needed to collect Social Security retirement benefits:

If you reach 62 in	You need to have worked this many years*
1985	8½
1986	8¾
1987	9
1988	9¼
1989	9½
1990	9¾
1991 or later	10

Source: Social Security Administration
*One year equals 4 separate quarters

For most of us, all of our working lives will count toward our "number of years worked." For those of you who work for nonprofit organizations, however, Social Security added you to their coverage on January 1, 1984. Only employment for those years since that date will be used in figuring benefits, unless you have been paying Social Security taxes all along.

If you are older than 55 and work for a nonprofit organization, you can qualify for benefits if you can work up to 5 more years (the actual number of quarters needed is dependent on your age at January 1, 1984).

Early Retirement Will Cost You

As you may know, if you currently retire at age 65, you will receive full benefits: if you retire earlier, you will receive only a percentage of your full benefits. For each month that you receive Social Security benefits prior to age 65, your monthly benefit will be permanently reduced. If you are 62 and elect to receive benefits, you will receive 20% less than what your full benefit would have been.

For each month you wait to take benefits after you reach age 62, the reduction will be less. Your retirement benefit will be reduced by 5/9 of 1% for each month you receive it before age 65. The actual formula for determining the reduction amount (amount your full benefit will be reduced) is this:

5/9 × 1/100 × unreduced benefit × months before age 65.

For example, if you retired at age 64 (12 months before age 65) and your unreduced monthly benefit would have been $400, the amount by which your benefit will be reduced is figured this way: 5/9 × 1/100 × $400 × 12 = $26.67. So you would receive $373.33 (or $400.00 − $26.67). Similar formulas apply for figuring the benefits of the spouse, the widow, or the widower of a worker.

Retirement Age Rising

As you may also know, the Social Security law was amended in 1983 to gradually increase the age at which a worker can retire to receive full benefits. The following table indicates how this age will increase:

Year of birth	Year you are 62	Age for full benefits
1937 or earlier	1999 or earlier	65 years
1938	2000	65 years, 2 months
1939	2001	65 years, 4 months
1940	2002	65 years, 6 months
1941	2003	65 years, 8 months
1942	2004	65 years, 10 months
1943–1954	2005–2016	66 years
1955	2017	66 years, 2 months
1956	2018	66 years, 4 months
1957	2019	66 years, 6 months
1958	2020	66 years, 8 months
1959	2021	66 years, 10 months
1960 or later	2022 or after	67 years

Later Retirement—It May Pay

You may not want to give up working at age 65 (or whatever age you would normally receive full benefits). If you do continue working and delay receiving Social Security payments, you will end up with increased monthly benefits when you do retire.

If you were born in the years 1917 through 1924, each month you delay retirement you will receive a 0.25% increase—3% a year—in your benefit. For those of you born in 1925 or later, your benefit will be increased between 3½% and 8% a year depending on how long after 1924 you were born. (The rise equates to one-half of one percent every other year until it reaches 8% for those born in 1943.)

In addition, because of the way Social Security benefits are calculated, you could well end up with an increase in your basic benefit, even before the delayed retirement credit is added. Briefly, your monthly benefit is calculated on an average monthly wage. The average monthly wage is figured on a certain number of years of earnings. By working longer, you can replace early years of lower earnings with later years of presumably higher income for the calculation of the average monthly wage, thereby increasing that amount.

Combine Social and Employment Security

If you decide to work while you are collecting Social Security retirement benefits, your benefits could be cut. Since the basic purpose of Social Security is to provide income for workers and families where earnings have been eliminated or substantially reduced, your monthly check could be slashed if you earn over a minimum threshold, called the annual exempt amount.

For 1985, the annual exempt amount was $7,320 for a person between the ages of 65 and 70, and $5,400 for someone under age 65. The same figures for 1986 are $7,800 and $5,760 respectively—the amounts are raised annually according to the increase in the cost of living. Should your earnings go over this threshold, your benefits are reduced $1 for every $2 you earn over the minimum. Beginning in 1990, this penalty will be reduced; after that, benefits will be cut $1 for every $3 earned over the minimum. Once you reach age 70, however, your Social Security benefits will no longer be reduced due to other earnings (prior to 1983, this age was 72).

If you are going to earn more than the minimum plus twice your Social Security, you are not only ahead of the game, but you probably should defer taking Social Security payments until you stop working.

More Details

In addition to the yearly minimum, a monthly minimum test can also be used. There are exceptions, but this method is generally available only once—in the year of retirement. You can collect in the months that your earnings do not exceed the annual minimum divided by 12—this allows you to collect Social Security benefits in the year you retire, even if your earnings prior to retirement would have exceeded the annual minimum.

What Constitutes Earnings

For an employee, gross wages (not just take-home pay) count as earnings. Included in wages are any bonuses, commissions, vacation pay, cash tips of $20 or more in a month and the value of noncash items such as meals or living quarters. Excluded from wages are investment and interest income, capital gains, Social Security benefits, and income from pensions and other retirement plans, and, in most cases, rental income from real estate.

If you do have income while you're receiving Social Security payments, you must file an annual report of earnings with the Social Security Administration by April 15 of the following year. If you suspect that you will earn over the annual exempt amount, you should also notify Social Security so they can reduce your monthly payments if necessary. If you receive more than you are entitled to in any year, you may be required to repay that amount. Remember, too, that you still may have to pay income taxes on your earnings, no matter how old you are.

This COLA Is Not a Drink

You are assured, by law, of getting cost-of-living adjustments (COLAs) in your otherwise fixed Social Security benefits. Currently, when the cost of living, as measured by the Consumer Price Index (CPI), is 3% or more, your payment is adjusted accordingly. If the CPI rises by less than 3%, there is no adjustment.

No Minimums But a Nice Maximum

In prior years, the law allowed for a minimum Social Security payment, but it was eliminated. Now it is possible to be eligible for a small amount of benefits if your earnings have been very low. For the 1985 year, the maximum monthly primary insurance amount for a person retiring at age 65 was $739. A person who retired in that year at a later age (having worked longer) could receive a considerably higher amount.

Benefits for Your Family

Depending on the age of the worker, benefits are payable to spouses or divorced spouses, children, widows or widowers, and, in certain cases, dependent grandchildren and parents.

A nonworking (for pay) spouse or divorced spouse of a worker can receive as much as one-half of the worker's benefit. Similarly, your children, if you are retired, may receive a payment of 50% of your benefit, or 75% should you die, until your child is 18 years old. Under prior law, this benefit could be continued until age 22 if your child was attending college, but subsequent legislation significantly tightened payments over the age of 18. Should you die, your spouse is eligible to receive a retirement benefit of 75% of your primary insurance amount at age 60, or age 50 if he or she is severely disabled.

How Much Will You Get

Until now we have ignored how to estimate what your benefits might be. It is not a simple process. You need to know in detail your earnings history, and then apply some quite complicated formulas. Rather than go into that here, we have provided the table on the next page, useful for estimating your benefits.

How to Get Your Benefits

The Social Security Administration will not automatically send you your benefits on your 65th birthday. You must contact the nearest Social Security office if you wish to make a claim. If you call the office first, you will be told what records you need to bring with you to arrange for benefits.

Remember that you can arrange for easy direct deposit of your

Social Security check into your bank, thrift institution, and many money market funds. Just call your bank or fund and ask. If it can't arrange for direct deposit from the Treasury Department, all you have to do is have your check sent directly to the fund. Have the check addressed so that it is payable to your money fund account.

Even if you are planning on working beyond age 65 and deferring your Social Security benefits, you should still contact the Social Security Administration prior to your 65th birthday so that your eligibility for Medicare benefits can be established. (Medicare is covered in Chapter 10.)

Estimated Monthly Social Security Benefits

Taxing Matters

As mentioned earlier you will have to pay income taxes on any employment earnings you have if you work past 65, no matter what your age. Social Security payments were previously exempt from

Your Age In 1987	Your Present Annual Earnings and Prospective Monthly Benefits				
	$10,000	$16,000	$23,000	$31,000	$40,000+
65	$ 382	$ 522	$ 665	$ 698	$ 717
64	392	533	679	716	737
63	398	541	691	730	754
62	403	547	698	741	767
61	404	548	701	744	773
55–60	406	552	705	753	789
51–55	410	558	712	771	820
46–50	414	565	720	793	858
41–45	395*	540*	685*	768*	844*
31–40	396*	543*	683*	775*	869*
Under 31	386*	530*	663*	753*	850*

The table assumes steady employment and average pay increases.
*These amounts have been reduced for early retirement at age 65; the "normal" retirement age is higher for these workers.
Source: William M. Mercer-Meidinger Inc.

income taxes (through 1983), but now up to one-half of your benefits could be subject to federal income taxes. (See "Taxes and Retirement" in Chapter 1.)

Only about 10% of today's retirees pay income taxes on part of their Social Security checks, but by the time today's 20 to 40 year olds reach retirement age, an estimated 50% of them will find their benefits being taxed away. All the more reason to begin investing in your own retirement plan.

Individual Retirement Accounts

Between 1981 and 1986, taxpayers got a real boost: They could make tax-deductible contributions to Individual Retirement Accounts (IRAs). Investment earnings on the accounts were tax-free until retirement. More than 40 million people took advantage of this boon, accumulating IRA assets of over $170 billion.

IRAs became a major target of tax reformers. However, voters liked the opportunity to help themselves to a comfortable retirement too much to let this valuable tax break be taken away. TC '86 still allows everybody with earned income to have an IRA, and still allows investment earnings to go untaxed until the IRA owner begins to withdraw the funds. However, the new rules (which go into effect for the 1987 tax year) keep people with certain income levels from deducting IRA contributions on their tax returns—employees who participate in a company-sponsored retirement plan can still maintain an IRA account and put money in it each year. However, the new rules say that —depending on income level—workers may not get a tax deduction for their contributions.

The adoption of the new tax code means that the IRA, once an invaluable cornerstone in every working person's financial plan, is still a useful tool—but no longer an automatic recommendation. However, even if you don't qualify for the IRA deduction, it helps that your investments can still grow tax-free until retirement. So, you may want to keep contributing to your IRA in any case. But assess all your options. You might do better by investing in other retirement savings plans, or using the money you would otherwise place in your IRA to beef up your investment portfolio.

Who Can Open an IRA

You can open an IRA, or make contributions to an existing IRA, as long as you are under the age of 70½ and have any income from "compensation." Compensation includes wages, salaries, professional fees, tips, commissions, bonuses, alimony, and income from self-employment. Compensation does not include interest income, dividends, rent from property or pension or annuity payments. If you earn less than $2,000, the most you can contribute is your entire compensation.

If both you and your spouse are employed, each of you can have an IRA, but if only one of you works for compensation, the working spouse can set up a small separate "spousal" IRA.

Annual Investment Limits

Strictly speaking, there is no minimum investment requirement, though some plan custodians may require a minimum initial investment in the neighborhood of $500. Your maximum contributions, however, for each year are set by law: $2,000 per person (a total of $2,250 for a worker and his or her unemployed spouse) or 100% of your compensation for the year, whichever is less. If both you and your spouse have earned at least $2,000 employment income each, you can each contribute $2,000 to an IRA for a total of $4,000— deductible from your taxable income. If you are divorced, and your working spouse had set up a spousal IRA for you while you were still married, you can now contribute as much as permitted for an ordinary IRA—$2,000—if you are receiving alimony (considered to be compensation, you earned it) or have your own earned income.

Contribution Time Limits

You do not have to make contributions to your IRA all in one lump sum—you can invest gradually as your funds are available. Of course you should realize that the earlier you contribute, the more you will earn in the long run; in other words, the sooner you get your money in, the sooner you will be earning on it.

You do actually have 15½ months in which to invest in your IRA for any one particular tax year. You can invest on January 1 or on April 15 of the following tax year. If you do wait until April 15 to fund your IRA, that doesn't mean that you have to wait that long to file your tax return with the IRS. Liberalized laws now allow you to file your tax return earlier and indicate what amount you will contribute by April 15, applicable to the previous tax year. In fact, if you file early enough, and receive a tax refund before April 15, you can use your refund toward your IRA contribution. But if you do not make the contribution to your IRA as you promised the IRS, you could be subject to penalties and additional taxes.

IRA Deductions

People who are self-employed, or employees who are not participants in qualified pension plans, can continue to use the IRA rules that were in effect before the new tax law was implemented. However, employees who are plan participants (even if their benefits are not vested) will find that the IRA deduction is phased out (reduced), according to their adjusted gross income. A 401(k) "cash or deferred arrangement" or a Keogh counts as a qualified plan for this purpose.

If either spouse is a plan participant, the other spouse is also affected by the phase-out rules. The deductible amount that workers can deposit in a spousal IRA for a nonworking spouse is also phased out according to income.

The full $2,000 deduction is allowed for an individual with an adjusted gross income under $25,000 and a married couple filing a joint return with an adjusted gross income under $40,000. (Married people who file separate returns *never* qualify for the full $2,000 IRA deduction.) The deduction is phased out completely (with a dollar of deduction lost for every five dollars of income), until single taxpayers with AGI over $35,000 and married joint filers with AGI over $50,000 lose the deduction entirely. (Remember, nondeductible contributions are still permitted.)

However, there's a special "floor" on the deduction: If you qualify for any deduction at all, you can take a deduction of $200. For example, if you'd theoretically be eligible for a $130 deduction, you can claim $200. Moreover, the deduction is rounded down to the next lowest $10 amount. That is, if you'd otherwise qualify for a deduction of $1,247, you claim $1,240.

What Investments Can You Use

Now that you have raised the money, what can you invest your IRA funds in? There are many, many ways your funds can be invested. In general, your IRA can be set up with a bank, savings and loan institution, insurance company, mutual fund family, or stock brokerage firm as your trustee. Your IRA must have a trustee owing to rules regarding fiduciary and financial responsibility, periodic audits, and other matters. Thus you as an individual cannot be trustee of your own account.

As you can probably tell, the specific investments allowed are even greater than the number of trustees you can choose. The only major investments *not* allowed for an IRA are so-called hard assets such as precious metals, gemstones, works of art, antiques, and other collectibles. Note: The new tax law allows you to invest your IRA funds in gold coins issued by the U.S. government.

The Tax Code of '86 completely changed the way investors think about IRA investment. Before the new law, capital gains (such as profits on the sale of stock) got treatment more favorable than ordinary income (e.g., salary; interest on a CD). Thus, IRA owners used to be cautious about putting growth investments into an IRA, because they felt that they would be taking profits that would otherwise qualify for favorable capital gains treatment, and paying higher ordinary-income rates once they began IRA withdrawals.

The new tax law more or less eliminates the distinction between capital gains and ordinary income. That makes growth investments more attractive for your IRA—but remember that high potential for growth usually means high risk of loss if you act without the benefit of expert advice. Some people's investment philosophy is that they have plenty of time to catch up and wait for "slow learner" stocks to catch on. It's the old buy-hold-pray approach. Other investors insist on absolute safety in IRA investment because they know they'll need the money for retirement. Finally, there are those who learn how to assume an appropriate level of investment risk as they seek maximum potential rewards from growth stock investments. (Chapter 8 describes the Donoghue Strategy for achieving strong, steady returns from growth stock investments and for avoiding loss.)

Another strategy using tax-exempts: If you don't qualify for an IRA deduction, you might not want to contribute to your IRA. Instead, use your spare funds to buy tax-exempt investments. You won't be taxed on the income, and there are no restrictions on the amount you can invest or when and how you withdraw the money. No tax deduction for the investment, of course—but if you don't qualify for an IRA deduction, you have nothing to lose by doing this.

Deciding Where to Invest

So far, we have only really discussed where you cannot invest. When you start looking into where to invest, you could become overwhelmed by all the choices available. To make matters more complicated, you need not invest all your IRA funds with a single custodian—you can split them up.

One caveat, though, is that each trustee will typically charge you a fee to maintain your IRA and the more trustees you have, the more expensive your IRA program becomes. (Moreover, it's generally a good idea to pay the fee directly than have it deducted from your account. Keep *all* your IRA money earning tax-deferred profits.)

Banks and Savings and Loan Institutions

Currently, the bulk of IRA money is in banks and savings and loans (see chart below), though these institutions' share of IRA deposits has been shrinking from year to year. These institutions offer certificates of deposit (CDs) with fixed or variable rates and money market deposit accounts (MMDAs). Banks heavily promote their convenience and federal deposit insurance for accounts up to $100,000. But MMDAs typically underperform even money market mutual funds. Worse, certificates of deposit can carry substantial penalties should you want to make a switch when a more attractive opportunity presents itself (for example, if you are in a fixed rate CD and interest rates are going up). To counter their declining market share, some banks and S&Ls are now offering mutual funds and self-directed accounts. (A self-directed account allows you to choose your investments, for example, specific stocks and bonds, subject to trading commissions.)

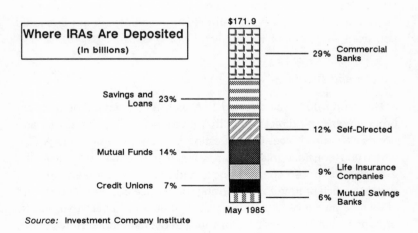

Where IRAs Are Deposited
(In billions)

$171.9

Savings and Loans 23%

Mutual Funds 14%

Credit Unions 7%

29% Commercial Banks

12% Self-Directed

9% Life Insurance Companies

6% Mutual Savings Banks

May 1985

Source: Investment Company Institute

Insurance Firms

Insurance companies also offer investments in the form of annuities. A fixed annuity is similar to a bank CD. You can open an account with a minimum amount and add to it periodically. Typically, the rate at which you start investing would be guaranteed for a year, and after that adjusted at the insurer's discretion. Your only "guarantee" of principal is the insurance company itself and its financial health. Should you choose to go this route, you'd be well advised to invest with a major company with a top rating from *Best's Insurance Reports* (available at most libraries).

Variable annuities are essentially mutual funds, invested in stocks or bonds and typically managed by the insurer. As is characteristic of a mutual fund, your return will vary according to the performance of the underlying securities. You will usually be allowed to switch among funds, but may well be assessed a fee for each switch. (See the section on annuities below.)

Keep in mind, also, that insurance companies will charge a fee—either a sales fee or a surrender fee—when you get out of the annuity. As mentioned before, early withdrawal penalties can apply should you want to shift your investment.

Stocks and Bonds

By setting up a self-directed IRA with a full service or discount broker, you can "direct" your IRA investments into the stocks and bonds of your choice. One question you should ask yourself first when you consider this option is whether you feel you have the expertise to choose specific stocks and bonds, and are you able to devote sufficient time to monitoring them once bought? You should always be aware of any developments that could affect your stocks or bonds—either individually or through overall market movements.

On the plus side for stocks, most are liquid—easily bought and sold —and can provide protection from inflation since corporate profits and dividends reflect the impact of inflation, albeit at a slightly lagged pace. However, the tricky part is choosing *good* investments, not just relying on someone's hot tip or the fad of the day, and timing the purchase and sale of your shares. Of course, if you use a full service brokerage firm, you are paying your stockbroker to provide you with guidance. If you are using a discount brokerage, you have to rely on your own judgment.

Bonds

On the surface, bonds may appear very attractive. They pay interest semi-annually and often sport yields greater than those of money funds. But bonds can hold pitfalls you may not be aware of. The minimum purchase amount is typically $1,000, and the commission for a purchase or sale will be at least $25 per $1,000 bond, though that percentage falls gradually with higher purchases. Bond prices tend to be quite volatile—they respond inversely to changes in interest rates. Thus, should you purchase a bond in times of rising interest rates, you will be losing money—at least on paper—on the price of your bond. On the other hand, should interest rates fall, you could achieve very attractive capital gains, provided you sell before rates change direction again.

There are a number of types of bonds, from high-grade corporate bonds (issued by the most financially strong companies) to so-called junk bonds (those with no ratings or very low credit ratings) to convertible bonds (convertible into common stock).

One other relatively new type of bond is the zero-coupon bond. Introduced in 1981, they have grown rapidly in popularity as IRA investments. Zero-coupon bonds are bought at a huge discount from face value, and while you hold it you do not receive any interest payments—hence the name zero coupon. Rather, the "interest" you receive consists of the difference between what you get when you cash in the bond at maturity and what you paid for it. Outside an IRA, you would be taxed each year as if you were receiving interest all along, but when you hold one in an IRA your earnings are tax-deferred, hence you avoid an otherwise unpalatable tax treatment.

Because you do not receive periodic interest, however, you cannot reinvest those monies as with a regular bond. In addition, the price of zero-coupon bonds can fluctuate more than that of a regular bond.

Gold and Real Estate

While we stated above that these were not suitable IRA investments, in certain forms they are allowed, and deserve a brief mention. You can invest in the stock of corporations involved in the mining, processing and sale of gold and other precious metals; or in a mutual fund which focuses on such investments. You must bear in mind that gold has historically been a very volatile commodity, but it does have a function as a store of value, and can prove a savvy investment should inflation suddenly surge or some crisis rock the world economies. Still, as we advise readers of Donoghue's MONEYLETTER®, no more than 5% of your investment should be in this medium.

Real estate, if mortgaged, is not permitted for an IRA investment. That restricts you to using cash to purchase a real estate investment for your IRA, which would most likely tie up a great deal of your IRA money. One other drawback to using real estate as an IRA investment is that a number of benefits that make real estate an attractive investment outside an IRA (such as depreciation write-offs, mortgage interest deductions and other tax deductions) are not applicable inside an IRA. Furthermore, real estate is highly illiquid—not easily sold, and must often be held for a number of years to realize any significant price appreciation.

Still, there are two feasible ways to get real estate into your IRA. These are limited partnerships and real estate investment trusts (REITs). Limited partnerships basically involve a group of investors who pool their funds to buy properties or make mortgages. A sponsor or general partner usually will put such an arrangement together. Limited partnerships are sold most often through financial planners and brokerage firms. Before investing in a limited partnership, read and carefully evaluate the prospectus—check for the experience of the sponsors, the fairness of the contract, and what the guaranteed minimum return is before the partner gets a share. Keep in mind that it is very difficult to sell shares in a limited partnership (unless it is publicly traded), and most limited partnerships have built-in lives of five to ten years.

A REIT is a publicly traded company; you buy shares in its stock on one of the stock exchanges. The REIT essentially uses its shareholders' money to invest in real estate properties or to make mortgages. By law, a REIT must pay out 95% of its income from its investment properties—be they mortgages or rental income—and if the REIT sells a property, it passes gains on to shareholders in the form of extra earnings or a special dividend. Because shares of REITs are publicly traded, they are easily bought and sold.

Mutual Funds

Mutual fund families come in two forms—load and no-load—those that charge a sales commission and those that do not. Today, we even have funds with back-end loads (a fee when you sell your shares) and low-loads (small commissions of typically 1% to 3%).

We believe that no-load mutual fund families are the most attractive way for the majority of IRA investors to manage their funds. This is where the most investment flexibility can be found. Within the family, you can find a menu of mutual funds to suit your investment needs as they change over time. And whatever mutual fund you pick, you are getting the benefits of professional management and broad diversification, which may be difficult, if not impossible, to achieve on your own. This diversification reduces your risk—compare a broadly diversified stock portfolio of a mutual fund with the limited number of stocks you can invest in on your own, especially if you are just starting your IRA.

Mutual funds fall basically into three categories: money market mutual funds, stock funds, and bond funds. Of course, within these three basic groups are a number of different, more specialized funds.

Money Market Funds

These funds invest in money market instruments that are typically not available to the average investor. By investing in short term debt securities of the highest quality, money market funds are unique among mutual funds in that their net asset value per share is constant and is usually $1.00. This provides you with safety of principal. Money market mutual funds are not guaranteed like bank offerings, but no one, to our knowledge, has ever lost money in a money fund. And no money fund has ever invested in an obligation that failed to pay off at maturity.

Stock Funds

These funds can fall into a number of categories based on the stated objective of the particular fund. In general, they all invest in common, preferred, or convertible stocks. They can be classified as follows:

- aggressive growth funds—seeking bargain-priced stocks that will later soar in value, they typically rise faster than the overall stock market in an up market, but fall faster in a down market.
- growth funds—more conservative than the above, but still looking for stocks whose prices grow significantly.
- growth and income funds—they look for stocks that will grow in value, but also pay healthy dividends. Usually this balance is found in large, mature corporations.

Bond Funds

Bond mutual funds can invest in a wide variety of obligations, or they can invest in a specific type of bond. For example, a fund can invest in government securities only, high-grade corporate bonds, low-quality junk bonds, zero-coupon bonds or government agency bonds like GNMAs (Ginnie Maes, obligations of the Government

National Mortgage Association). As with straight bonds, bond funds also move in response to changes in interest rates, and can be quite volatile.

A somewhat hybrid bond investment is the unit investment trust. Really an unmanaged mutual fund, the trust can invest in a wide range of securities, but all obligations purchased mature on the same date, and once purchased, the portfolio is fixed. Investors typically buy units of $1,000, and while there is a sales fee (usually about 3%), the yield on the trust is quoted after that fee is taken into account. The sponsor of the trust is willing to buy your units back from you at current market value, although that market value will fluctuate in response to interest rates. This means that if you decide to switch into another IRA investment at the wrong time in the interest rate cycle, you'll suffer a loss of principal.

Stock and Bond Funds

A number of mutual funds invest in a combination of stocks and bonds, seeking a combination of primarily high income and some capital appreciation. They might hold 100% stocks or bonds, or any combination thereof. Typically, such funds are described as balanced funds or income funds. Balanced funds, as the name suggests, divide their portfolio holdings between stocks and bonds according to set ratios.

(For further information on these and other types of investments, and investment strategies, refer to Chapters 7 and 8.)

Overenthusiasm Can Cost You

What happens if, by accident, you contribute more than the maximum allowed into your IRA for a particular year? If you catch your mistake before you file your tax return for the year, you can simply remove the excess contribution.

The IRS, as you might guess, will not allow you to deduct an excess contribution for the tax year in which you made it. Furthermore, if you leave that excess in your IRA, it is subject to a 6% penalty tax for every year it remains in the IRA. What's more, if you decide to retrieve that amount from your IRA at any time, any income or interest it has earned will be taxed twice—as regular income and subject to a 10% premature distribution penalty. DON'T DO IT!

Strategic Recourses

If you overcontribute there are a few options that may be available. Instead of withdrawing the money and getting hit with double and punitive taxation, you could pay the 6% penalty on the extra amount for the first year, and then deduct that excess contribution as part of next year's IRA contribution. Just be sure that the rest of your contribution for the next year, when added to the extra for the previous year, does not exceed the maximum allowed.

If you already filed your tax return, and subsequently discover your excess contribution, you can file a form 1040X (to amend a tax return) and reassign the contribution to the next tax year, or take a distribution if you make the request before the April 15 deadline.

In any case, if you do find yourself in an excess contribution situation, you can always consult your tax adviser or the trustee of your IRA to determine the steps you can take to correct the situation.

Getting at Your Money Before Retirement

There are ways to get at your IRA money before you turn 59½, which is when you are first able to withdraw without penalty. Unfortunately, in most cases, it will cost you. If you withdraw money from your IRA before you are 59½, you will not only pay current taxes on it, you will also be assessed a nondeductible 10% tax penalty on the amount withdrawn.

Rollovers Are Easy

There is a way you can temporarily withdraw all or part of your IRA assets and not be penalized. By using a rollover, you take money out and have 60 days to use it before putting it back into an IRA. If you fail to put that money back within this time period, you are taxed as described in the paragraph above—at your current tax rate plus the 10% tax penalty.

You can use the rollover only once every twelve months. Your IRA's trustee will file a report of your rollover with the IRS, and if you attempt a rollover again before twelve months are up, the IRS will view it as a fully taxable withdrawal. In any case, income earned on the withdrawn amount must be included in your gross income when you file your annual tax return.

You can also use a rollover simply to change trustees and investments—for example, from one mutual fund family to another. In either case, the mechanics of a rollover are as follows.

You first write to the trustee of your IRA and request that you be sent a distribution in the amount you want to roll over, whether that be all or only a portion of your account. When you write, be sure to state that you plan to roll those funds over and want withholding taxes waived. Otherwise, the trustee may collect the 10% penalty tax on premature distributions. Once you receive the money, you have 60 days to use it before it must be redeposited into an IRA.

Rollover Warnings

Even if you miss the deadline—and it is not your fault—the IRS will most likely penalize you all the same. If you've suddenly found that you missed the 60-day deadline by only a couple of days, you could make matters worse by trying to sneak by and reinvest the funds at that time. Not only are you subject to ordinary income tax and the 10% penalty, but the IRS may well view any amount of that reinvestment over the maximum $2,000 annual contribution as an excess contribution, subject to that 6% a year excise tax.

Sometimes a Transfer Is Easier

If you do not wish to use your IRA funds for the 60-day period, but simply want to change your IRA investment, a direct transfer of funds may be preferable, at least on paper. In a direct transfer, you never touch your money, and thus can avoid the risk of any tax hassles from the IRS.

Your first step is to fill out an application to set up an IRA account with the new trustee. Then, notify your current trustee, in writing, to transfer your assets to the new account. There are no deadlines to meet, and you can transfer your IRA funds as often as you wish. (Keep in mind, though, that each time you transfer you could be charged liquidation fees from your old account, as well as start-up fees in your new account.)

Unfortunately, some custodians move at a snail's pace when it comes to transferring your funds. It can take longer to transfer less liquid IRA assets, such as shares in a real estate limited partnership, because they must be converted to cash for the transfer. Moreover, paperwork can be complicated unless full and clear instructions are given.

While these are legitimate reasons for slowing a transfer, at times the trustee just may not want to give up the funds. Horror stories abound concerning IRA transfers that took over one year to complete! Certainly, in hindsight, a rollover would have been quicker.

Tips to Tailor Transfers

Before you start to initiate a transfer, find out from your current sponsor how much you will owe in fees, both maintenance and liquidation, and find out how long it will take to transfer your investments. Generally speaking, liquid investments such as CDs, money market and other mutual funds, and actively traded stocks and bonds should be the fastest to transfer. Less liquid assets such as annuities, limited partnerships, and zero-coupon bonds could take longer to transfer. Have the fortitude to keep after the current trustee to get your assets transferred if necessary. If you are dissatisfied with the service, by all means complain—first to a branch manager and then to a regional manager.

Rollovers From Your Company Plan

One other type of rollover is available to you. Should you leave a job and take your pension benefit in the form of a lump-sum distribution, you can roll it over into your IRA within 60 days, with no tax consequences. It is a good idea, though, to keep this IRA separate from the one in which you make your annual contributions. (See Chapter 9.)

You do not, however, have to roll over your entire distribution if you don't want to. Should you decide to buy a retirement condo in Florida with part of your lump-sum distribution, whatever portion of the distribution you don't spend can still be rolled over into an IRA. Of course, whatever portion you do spend is includable in your taxable income for the year.

If you only receive a partial distribution from a qualified retirement plan, you may or may not be able to roll it over into an IRA. If that partial distribution is not part of a series of periodic payments, and is at least 50% of your total accrued benefits, you should be allowed to roll it over into an IRA when you retire.

Withdrawals Made Easy

As discussed earlier, withdrawals prior to age 59½ are subject to ordinary income taxes and a 10% tax penalty. If you are disabled, you are allowed to withdraw all of your IRA funds with no penalty tax, though you will have to pay current income taxes on the amount you withdraw.

Otherwise, you can begin taking withdrawals at age 59½, even if you are still working. On the other hand, you can also still make ˜ontributions at that age. But in the year following the year you turn 70½, you must begin taking distributions out of your IRA. When you turn 70½, you must cease making contributions.

Start Withdrawing at Age 70½

If you fail to remove money from your IRA by April 1 of the year following the year in which you turn 70½, you will be subjected to a severe 50% penalty tax on the amount you should have withdrawn. This minimum withdrawal amount is equal to the total amount of money you have accumulated in your IRA divided by your life expectancy (as determined by the IRS life expectancy tables). The Secretary of the Treasury may waive that 50% tax if your failure to withdraw was due to reasonable error and if reasonable steps are being taken to correct the situation.

Live With It or "Lump" It

You have two main choices for withdrawing your IRA money. First, you can withdraw the total amount in a "lump-sum payment." In this case, though, you will be taxed immediately on that entire amount; there is no five-year forward averaging tax preference like that permitted with some other types of retirement plans. Should you decide to invest some of your distribution outside an IRA, you will be taxed on those earnings.

Instead, it may be a good idea to remove your funds on a gradual payout schedule. In this manner, you will be taxed each year on only the amount you have withdrawn, and the amount remaining in your IRA will continue to earn tax-deferred income. There's also a 15% excise tax on excessively large withdrawals, but we suspect you won't have to worry: This means withdrawals over $112,500 a year.

A general rule of thumb in withdrawing funds—to insure that you will have funds as long as you are alive—is to withdraw an annual percentage of your IRA that is no greater than the rate at which the IRA is growing, i.e., the rate of return on your IRA. Should you wish to withdraw faster, you can tell by looking at the table opposite how long your money will last given the rate it is growing and the rate you are withdrawing.

If you do wait until you are 70½ to begin withdrawing, you will lose some flexibility because you must withdraw according to the IRS life expectancy tables. There are separate tables for single persons and for couples; the latter takes into account statistics that show that married people live longer than single people do. If you'd like the entire set of life expectancy tables, they are available in IRS *Publication No. 575, Pension and Annuity Income.* Call your regional IRS office for a copy.

How Long Will Your Money Last?

Annual Withdrawal	Annual Rate of Return				
	8%	9%	10%	11%	12%
9%	28 years	—*	—	—	—
10%	20	26	—	—	—
11%	16	19	25	—	—
12%	14	15	18	23	—
13%	12	13	15	17	21
14%	11	11	13	14	17
15%	9	10	11	12	14

*A dash indicates that the IRA will never run out.

What Happens When You Depart This Life

Although we do not like to think about it, there is a possibility that we could die before we begin to take distributions or after we have begun to withdraw. What happens then?

To make sure that your IRA passes smoothly to a chosen heir if you should die, when you open your IRA, name at least one beneficiary. You can always change your beneficiary later on. If you fail to name a beneficiary, your IRA might go into probate. It depends on state law. Your IRA will be considered as part of your taxable estate.

Your Beneficiary Has Choices

If you die prior to making any withdrawals, and assuming your spouse is your beneficiary, he or she would have two choices. First, your spouse can leave the account in your name, but then would be unable to withdraw any funds from it until the year in which you would have turned 59½ without incurring an early withdrawal penalty. He or she would have to begin withdrawing by April 1 of the year following the year you would have reached 70½. Your spouse's second choice would be to roll over your IRA accumulation into his or her own IRA. In that case, your spouse could begin withdrawing from the IRA when he or she reaches 59½. See our explanation of rollovers above.

If you had already begun to take distributions from your IRA, then your spouse must continue taking payments at a rate at least as high as you would have been required, had you lived.

Your Children Have Different Choices

A whole different set of rules applies if your IRA is left to a child. Basically, if you have not taken any distributions yet, your child can elect to have those assets paid to him or her in small amounts over his or her life expectancy. But if the child does not begin taking payments within a year of your death, he or she would be forced to empty your account within five years, which could have harsh income tax effects. If you had begun to take funds out of the IRA, then your child will continue to receive payments from that account based on his or her own life expectancy.

Given the penalty taxes, it would be silly for you to respond to tax law changes by pulling money out of an existing IRA. So, the question is whether you should start an IRA or keep making contributions. If you're entitled to the full deductible contribution, the answer is probably "yes." It's still helpful to use the IRA as a way to combine tax savings today with sizable retirement funds in the future.

If you qualify for a small deduction, don't rush out to open an IRA just on this basis. Remember, the trustees' fees for maintaining the account may wipe out your tax savings. And if you don't qualify for any deduction, the choice is even tougher. "Know thyself" is a basic investment aphorism. If you know that discontinuing IRA contributions means that you'll step up your consumption or make unwise investments, by all means keep up IRA contributions. Forced savings are a lot better than no savings at all.

However, if you have a high level of self-discipline and a good history of investment success, it might make more sense to fortify your existing non-IRA portfolio, perhaps giving extra attention to tax-exempts. If you're worried that you'll use up the proceeds of your investment portfolio long before retirement, think about annuities.

Annuities

Annuities are another retirement savings tool available to everyone. While you can outlive the proceeds of your IRA or Keogh plan, annuities can provide guaranteed payments for your lifetime.

Get the Right Fit

We've already mentioned annuities as one of the investment choices open to IRA owners. People can also buy annuity contracts from insurance companies outside the IRA context. Premiums used to buy non-IRA annuities are not tax-deductible, but annuities offer a tax-free buildup of appreciation lasting until the annuity funds are withdrawn. Unlike IRAs, there is no limit on the amount you are permitted to invest in non-IRA annuity contracts. If you don't qualify for an IRA deduction, or if the deduction is disappointingly small, a non-IRA annuity could be a good choice for you. (Warning: Another similarity to IRAs is that annuities carry a 10% penalty tax on withdrawals before age 59½.)

In its most basic form, an annuity is an agreement between you and the issuing insurance company whereby they agree to pay you a specified amount each month for a specified time period in exchange for a defined one-time payment or payments over time. For example, you can, for a fixed one-time payment, buy an annuity to pay you $500 a month for twenty years or life, whichever is longer. Or you could pay in a defined amount each month for as long as you work and then withdraw a defined amount each month after you retire. There are so many annuities offered by different companies that you really should shop around and compare prices carefully to get the best deal.

People like annuities because they provide the added element of certainty in your retirement program. Knowing exactly what the monthly retirement check will be gives much more security to many individuals. You can put cash away in a deferred annuity while you're working, and build tax-deferred earnings to use when you retire. When you retire, you can use those or other funds to purchase an immediate annuity, which provides you income within one year of the date the contract is purchased. These are the two basic types of annuity as classified by payment—deferred payment and immediate payment.

Deferred Payment Annuities

With a deferred payment annuity, also called a retirement annuity, you receive no payments until at least one year, and often more than one year, after you have paid the premium. Because payments are deferred, this type of annuity is most often bought by younger persons as a retirement savings device. Although your payments to the deferred annuity are not tax-deductible, the earnings that compound on the annuity are free from taxes until income payments begin, or cash values are partially or wholly withdrawn.

You can purchase a deferred payment annuity with either a single premium (payment) or continuing payments (installment or annual premium). The latter can be either fixed or flexible. Payments for a fixed premium annuity are, as they sound, consistent over the entire time you pay. In contrast, if you purchase an annuity with flexible premiums, there is no requirement that you pay a specific premium amount in any one year.

If you purchase a deferred annuity, your payments are broken into two periods—the first period, in which you receive nothing or only dividends while interest accumulates; and the second period, in which the contract matures and you begin to receive income for life.

Should you decide to cancel the annuity contract during the first period, before you begin receiving payments, you can surrender the policy and receive a cash value for it. You will most likely receive a very low cash value, especially during the first few years of paying for the contract. Thus, it is wise to invest in a deferred payment annuity only if you truly believe that you will be able to leave the funds in the contract.

Loans from Your Deferred Annuity

As with life insurance policies, deferred income annuities often have some provision for loans. In addition, should you die before you reach retirement age, the annuity usually allows for some cash refund (typically the cash-surrender value) to be paid to a beneficiary you name.

When you retire, your annuity is actually applied to the purchase of an immediate payment annuity. The amount you will receive annually from that annuity will depend on the cash value of the contract when you retire and your age. The cash value, in turn, is dependent on the total amount of premiums you paid and when they were paid, as well as the interest rate the insurance company paid on your premiums.

The insurance company can pay at either a fixed or variable rate. The variable rate is more common today. With a variable rate, you are assured of a stated minimum interest rate, but above that minimum, the rate is based on some current market rate of investment return.

When you retire, you also have the option to take the cash value of the policy, or use that cash value to purchase your own immediate payment annuity.

Immediate Payment Annuity

To purchase an immediate payment annuity, you must purchase a single-premium annuity, which means that you pay in one rather substantial lump sum. This happens because this type of annuity provides you with income almost immediately—within one year of when you purchased the contract.

One of the first annuities to be issued was the straight life annuity: payments are based on actuarial tables of mortality rates. After you die, the insurance company won't make any further payments. Because of this, the yield on this type of annuity is higher than those available from other types of annuities. For this reason, many people are hesitant to purchase a straight life annuity because they fear they will die before what is "average" and therefore will not get back what they paid for in premiums. But, you might look on the bright side: should you outlive the "average" you will end up receiving more than what you paid for.

Another type of immediate annuity is the cash refund annuity. It provides you with a guaranteed life income and also provides that should you die before you receive payments equal to what you paid for the policy, your beneficiary will receive the balance of that price in a lump sum.

Similarly, an installment refund annuity will pay your beneficiary the remainder of installment payments that will make up the difference between what you paid and what you received prior to your death. Should no beneficiary survive you, your estate will receive a lump payment. In both cases, if you received payments at least equal to your purchase price, the insurance company has no further obligation.

Variable Rate Annuities

Many people, after they retire, find themselves living on fixed incomes. With the typical annuity, because the purchase price determines the amount of money available for payments, there is no adjustment available for cost-of-living increases. Thus, the variable rate annuity was born.

Basically, a variable rate annuity contract resembles a mutual fund. Most invest in a portfolio of common stocks on the assumption that common stock price performance will at least beat the upward trend of inflation. In theory, the annuity payments would increase as the buying power of the dollar decreases: in reality, however, the performance of common stocks has not always kept pace with inflation. Variable rate annuities may also invest in other instruments, such as bonds and money market obligations, and the return you receive is tied to the value of the underlying securities. The idea is that you can have some control over where YOUR annuity invests.

If you do follow an investment strategy (such as the one described in Chapters 7 and 8), then you should have a shot at building your annuity by managing the money actively. The other way to go, of course, is to ignore reality and keep your fingers crossed. Finally, remember that when you purchase a variable rate annuity, you are assuming the investment risk—the risk inherent in movements in the various markets. If you are a savvy investor, then a variable rate annuity may be sensible.

Taxes

When you begin to receive payments at retirement, a large portion of that annuity income is tax free because it is a return of capital you've already paid taxes on: premiums.

The rest of your payment consists of income earned on your premium; it is taxable. It seems difficult to tell exactly how much is new interest and how much is a return of principal. Therefore, the IRS has specified a method for determining the amount of your annual payment that is nontaxable. Ask your insurance agent to help you with the details.

General Advice and Cautions

No annuity should be purchased without first checking out the financial stability of the sponsoring insurance company. It is relatively simple to look up its rating published in *Best's Insurance Reports,* available at most public libraries. It's easy to do and could save you thousands over the long run. Avoid companies with low ratings.

As with other investments, you should not purchase a particular annuity on the basis of one person's recommendations, be that person a friend, broker, insurance agent or whatever. Carefully compare a number of annuities; look at fees, returns, and any other specifics.

The fees charged and returns provided, in particular, can vary greatly. Ask to see the company's track record, whether for fixed or variable rate annuities. In the case of the latter, you should check the performance of the funds' managers.

You should always base a decision as to which type of annuity contract to purchase first on your needs and second on the benefits you will receive versus the fees you will pay.

3   Corporate Goodies: Retirement Tools Employers Provide

Every once in a while, you have a rotten day at work. You reach a point where you're fed up, but you supress the urge to march into your boss's office shouting the frustrated worker's theme song: "Take This Job and Shove It!"

Great fantasy, lousy financial planning. The reality is that many corporations offer super retirement savings plans that are hard, if not impossible, to replace by working on your own. In this chapter, we'll look at the most popular corporate programs—401(k) plans, SEPs, ESOPs, PAYSOPs, pension and thrift programs—as well as strategies for getting the most bang for your tax-deferred buck.

401(k) Plans: The Next Best Thing to a Paid Vacation

The 401(k) retirement savings plan—also called a "salary reduction plan"—traces its roots to the tried-and-true corporate thrift program. The thrift program basically allowed workers to contribute to a special investment account, on an after-tax basis, with employers matching all or part of that contribution. In 1978, Section 401(k) was added to the Internal Revenue Code; "proposed regulations" followed in 1981 and the 401(k) plan we know today was born.

One remarkable feature of this new retirement plan allows workers to make contributions on a pretax basis. As we explain below, by taking what seems like a pay cut, you're actually getting one of the best tax shelters ever offered by Uncle Sam. (All you're really doing is deferring receipt of—and, hence, taxes on—your 401(k) money.) Adding frosting to the cake, both employee and employer contributions can earn investment income tax free until withdrawn. Like an IRA, the 401(k) gets the power of tax-deferred compounding working for you.

The 401(k) Bandwagon

Because the 401(k) permits pretax contributions at a rate that exceeds the maximum amount allowed for an IRA, the 401(k) has caught on like wildfire at large corporations. The maximum annual IRA contribution is $2,000 while the maximum annual 401(k) contribution is 25% of a worker's compensation or $7,000, whichever is less.

Between 1982 and 1985, the majority of Fortune 1000 companies established 401(k)s. (In general, companies with fewer than 400 employees have trouble finding financial institutions that will help them set up 401(k)s—banks, insurers, and mutual funds are focusing first on the biggest employers, since those accounts offer the most profit potential.) The large corporations already know that by offering 401(k)s they can sweeten the benefits pot and thereby attract top quality personnel. Best of all, when a corporation contributes to a 401(k) on behalf of employees, it can take a juicy tax deduction (worth up to 15% of annual compensation paid to workers participating in the company's defined contribution plans).

401(k) Defined

Named for a section in the Internal Revenue Code, the 401(k) plan is also known as a "cash or deferred" arrangement or, more commonly, as a salary reduction plan. By definition, the 401(k) plan is part of your employer's tax-qualified profit-sharing or stock bonus plan. While each company will design a plan to meet its own needs, there are three basic types of plans.

1. The *pretax thrift plan* is very popular with employees since employers match contributions. The generally accepted salary reduction amount for this plan is 6%.
2. Only employees contribute to the *salary reduction savings plan.* Your employer makes no matching contribution. The most common reduction in salary under this plan is 10%.
3. Similar to a pretax thrift plan, the *cash deferred profit-sharing plan* also has employers matching, to some extent, your contribution. The difference with this plan is that you can elect to take your employer's contribution in cash, if you wish. That cash distribution, however, will be taxed at ordinary income rates.

"Make Me a Match"

The majority of salary reduction plans do feature an employer matching contribution. A recent survey by Hewitt Associates, an employee benefits consulting firm, showed that 84% of plans surveyed did offer an employer matching contribution. In addition, the most common match is $0.50 for every $1.00 you put in up to 6% of your annual base compensation (see chart below). But that match varies from much less to amounts over $1.00 for every $1.00 you put in. Of the employers surveyed who did not offer a "match," 55% had an alternative form of employer contribution which was not based directly on the amount employees deferred from salary.

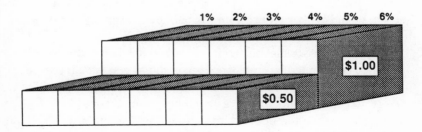

For every dollar you save each year through your 401(k),
your company may contribute 50 cents.

Legal Requirements

All 401(k) plans must meet certain guidelines to be "tax-qualified." The plan must be voluntary and must be nondiscriminatory (employees at the high end of the pay scale must not benefit disproportionately from those at the lower end). In addition, all of your contributions made to the 401(k), plus the earnings on those contributions, must be immediately 100% vested and nonforfeitable. Any contributions made by your employer to the plan need not be 100% vested immediately, but must be vested in accordance with ERISA (Employee Retirement Income Security Act of 1974) requirements. (See discussion of vesting rules for pension and profit-sharing plans later in this chapter.) All salary reduction plans must also meet other specifications applicable to any tax-qualified plan.

Employee Contributions

As explained earlier, the amount contributed to the 401(k) is a reduction in your annual salary that in turn reduces your related federal income tax bill. Here's how the typical plan works: you choose to reduce your salary by a certain percentage—generally between 2% and 10%. Assume that you put 5% of your monthly pay of $2,500 into a plan; you are actually reducing your monthly salary for tax purposes to $2,375 ($2,500 − $125). If you are in the 30% marginal tax bracket, you would be saving $37.50 a month, or $450 a year, in taxes. You could even use this savings to contribute to your IRA, which would further reduce your tax bill. (See Chapter 2 for details on IRAs.)

The Hewitt Associates survey found little difference in the percent of salary contributed by employees according to pay rate. In particular, it found that of employees participating in the 401(k) plan, the lower two-thirds on the pay scale contributed an average of 6.3% of their salary, while the upper third deferred an average of 7.4%.

If you can't afford to fund your 401(k) up to the maximum amount allowed by your company's plan, you might consider borrowing the money to do so. The Tax Code of 1986 has changed the rules about deductibility of interest, so that you will not necessarily get a tax deduction if you borrow to make up for the salary deferral. However, the point to remember is that if you plan properly, what you save on income taxes by contributing to a 401(k) could actually offset most of the interest charges. Not a bad deal!

Investments

Unlike many other company-sponsored retirement plans, you'll be given a choice of investment options for your 401(k) contributions. Your company's chief financial officer reviews the money management services offered by a host of financial institutions, then selects three or four from which you may choose. The menu of investment options available to 401(k) participants will probably include company stock, a common stock mutual fund, a money market mutual fund, a long-term bond mutual fund, or a guaranteed investment contract (GIC). Your company's CFO will try to cover all bases by offering a good assortment of investment approaches; he or she will see that there's something to suit everyone, from the very conservative to the more risk-oriented investor.

The Hewitt Associates study showed that 71% of the 401(k) plans surveyed offered three or more types of investment options. The three most common alternatives were an equity fund, a guaranteed investment contract and company stock. Over one-third of the plans offered bond or fixed income funds and short-term securities. Other alternatives included a balanced fund, life insurance, government securities, and real estate.

When the time comes to pick your 401(k) investment, you'll want to be sure that your choice is tailored to your individual goals and objectives. (See Chapters 7 and 8 for more details on investment strategies.) If you are relatively young, you can probably assume more risk and be more aggressive in your investing. An investment in company stock or an equity fund could build up nicely over the long haul. However, as you near retirement, you will probably want to alter your investment approach; perhaps you'll switch into a more conservative vehicle, such as a money market fund, that, by its very nature, seeks to preserve principal and provide regular income. One word of caution—if you think you may be leaving your job for another employer, you should probably keep your investments as liquid as possible so that your funds are easily accessible when you "separate from service." Tax treatment of such a distribution is discussed below.

Loans

Borrowing from your 401(k) plan must be done according to strict guidelines, which, if not met, will subject your "loan" to ordinary income taxes. For one thing, you may take out a plan loan if loans are available to all other participants equally. What's more, the loan must bear a reasonable rate of interest, established by the plan—for instance, the prime rate plus 1%.

The term of the loan cannot be longer than five years, with one exception. The exception is for loans to buy a principal residence. Rehab loans, and loans to buy a second or vacation home, don't qualify. Should you meet the five-year qualification at the time you take the loan, but later decide to extend payment beyond five years, the balance owed at the time you extend it will be treated as a taxable distribution at that time.

There is one other limit—the amount of loan you may take from your 401(k) plan. When you arrange for a loan, the amount of that loan, when added to the outstanding balance of all other loans you have taken, cannot exceed $50,000 or 50% of your nonforfeitable accrued benefit in the plan, whichever is less. If your loan pushes the total outstanding over this limit, it will be treated as a taxable distribution. You are allowed to borrow up to a $10,000 minimum, even if that amount is more than half of your nonforfeitable benefit.

However, despite the attractiveness of this loan provision, the majority of 401(k) plans do not offer loans. The Hewitt Associates survey showed that only 36% of 401(k) plans had a loan provision; of these, 15% required that employees satisfy some definition of "extreme hardship" before a loan would be granted. Most firms also limited the amount of loans that could be outstanding at one time or made in one year; they also had minimum loan amounts.

Plan Withdrawals

In addition to 401(k) loans, penalty-free withdrawals are permitted only under certain conditions: if you retire, die, become disabled, are separated from service, attain age 59½, or face financial hardship.

"Hardship" means immediate and heavy financial need, when funds are not available from other resources. TC '86 really tightens up the availability of hardship withdrawals from 401(k) plans. You can make a hardship withdrawal without penalty *only* to the extent that you withdraw your own deferred salary—not employer matching funds or income on money deferred in earlier years.

Tax Treatment of Distributions

Distributions from a 401(k) can be in the form of a lump sum or an annuity. When you make a hardship withdrawal, or when you receive payouts in the form of an annuity, the amount of the distribution is taxed as ordinary income in the year it is received.

When you take payment in the form of a lump-sum distribution, you have two basic options for avoiding the full brunt of taxes: special averaging provisions or a rollover.

Averaging rules: Pre-TC '86 law allowed plan participants who had been participants for at least five years before receiving a lump-sum distribution to improve their tax picture by using "ten-year forward averaging." Under this method for figuring tax, the lump sum is taxed in the year the participant receives it—*but* the tax is figured as if one-tenth of the distribution had been received in each of ten years. This is helpful because tax rates are lower on lower incomes. Under ten-year forward averaging, the tax equals ten times the income tax on one-tenth of the distribution, using the rate for single taxpayers (whatever the plan participant's marital status). Employees could also qualify for capital gains treatment on the part of the distribution that could be traced to certain contributions made to the pension plan before January 1, 1974. (Why that date? It's the effective date of ERISA, a major federal pension statute.)

However, TC '86 lowers tax rates and decreases the number of tax brackets, so averaging is less helpful. Anyway, TC '86 also restricts averaging to five years. The rules for five-year forward averaging are otherwise pretty much the same as those for ten-year forward averaging.

Before you get down in the mouth about the loss of ten-year forward averaging, check to see if you qualify to use it under a special transition rule in TC '86. If your fiftieth birthday arrived before January 1, 1986, you get a special one-time choice. If you get a lump-sum distribution, you can either use ten-year forward averaging (but pre-TC '86 tax rates) or five-year forward averaging (with the new rates). You can also take qualifying pre-1974 contributions out of the plan at a special 20% capital gains tax rate.

Rollovers. The second option you have is to use a rollover. With this method, you reinvest the proceeds of your plan, within 60 days, in (1) another qualified plan (if, say, you change employers) or (2) an IRA. Under normal circumstances, you must roll over the entire distribution. A partial rollover is permitted without tax penalties *only* if it is motivated by the employee's death, disability, or leaving the employer's service. Keep in mind that if you do roll over your distribution into an IRA, you will no longer be able to use ten-year forward income averaging on that amount.

Drawbacks and Benefits

Like most good things in life, there are some drawbacks to contributing to a 401(k). For starters, these contributions are reductions to your current salary—which may be hard to swallow if you're always short on cash. Moreover, contributions may, in effect, reduce the benefits you get from other company programs (this happens if those other goodies are pegged to your annual compensation). And, let's not forget, if you do participate in the 401(k) plan, your ability to withdraw funds is severely limited. Finally, you may be uncomfortable assuming responsibility for your 401(k) investment decisions.

Still, for most people, 401(k) plans are a great way to save for retirement. Not only do your contributions escape current taxation, but the earnings they achieve compound tax free. In all, this company-sponsored tax shelter lets you build up a substantial nest egg and frees you from being overly dependent on Social Security in your golden years.

Remember, the 401(k) outshines the IRA on five key points:

1. you can contribute far more each year to your 401(k) than your IRA.
2. your company will probably match your 401(k) contribution 50 cents on the dollar. (By refusing to participate in the 401(k) plan, you are, in effect, saying "no thanks" to a pay raise.)
3. your 401(k) plan may permit you to borrow money.
4. if you face a financial hardship, you can withdraw your own deferred salary without getting hit by a 10% penalty.
5. after retirement, you can withdraw 401(k) money in a lump sum and take advantage of the averaging rules and perhaps receive a special 20% capital gains tax rate on amounts contributed before 1974.

Simplified Employee Pensions

As the name suggests, the simplified employee pension, or SEP, was developed to give employers a "simplified" approach to retirement plans. The idea was to let employers offer retirement benefits and avoid the administrative requirements imposed by ERISA and the related cost burden. The SEP, which is technically a special type of IRA, was introduced by the Revenue Act of 1978.

Who Can Participate?

The SEP participation requirements are quite strict. The employer must include you in the plan if you (1) are at least 21 years old, (2) have worked for the employer for at least three of the past five calendar years, and (3) have earned at least $300 in compensation. The Internal Revenue Code does not specify that you must work a minimum number of hours during a calendar year, therefore, part-time employees are also included in the plan.

For the SEP to be legal, *all* employees must be included in the plan; your employer can insist, as a condition of employment, that you participate. (Certain union employees and nonresident aliens may be excluded.) If your employer does not demand that all employees participate in the SEP, and an eligible employee chooses not to participate, then no other employee can enter into the SEP agreement. Similarly, if one employee refuses to join the SEP, and your employer tries to establish a SEP with the rest of the employees, any contributions made by the employer to your account will not be considered tax-deductible SEP contributions.

For your employer to offer the choice of cash or SEP contributions described in the next paragraph, at least half the employees must choose to have funds contributed to the SEP.

Contribution Rules

Basically, your employer makes contributions to your IRA or individual retirement annuity. Your employer is not *required* to make any contribution to the SEP, but if a contribution is made to one employee's account, it must be made to all employees. In addition, it must meet nondiscrimination standards; in other words, your employer cannot discriminate in favor of the company's officers, shareholders, or highly paid employees.

Your employer must make contributions according to a set, written allocation formula. The formula can be changed from year to year, as long as the plan is amended by the date contributions must be made (that is, April 15 of the following year). The contributions limits for a regular SEP are either 15% of your compensation or $30,000, whichever is less. Beginning in 1988, the IRS will adjust the $30,000 figure to deal with changes in the cost of living. You can still maintain your own IRA if you're a SEP participant. However, the SEP is a qualified plan, so you will be subject to the rules about IRA deductions already described in Chapter 2.

TC '86 adds a new kind of plan for employers with 25 or fewer employees: the salary-reduction SEP. The employees can choose between receiving cash and "elective deferrals" (amounts deferred from salary and contributed to the SEP). The limit on these "elective deferrals," like the limit under 401(k) plans, is $7,000 a year.

Excess Contributions

What happens if your employer makes a contribution to your SEP over what you are allowed to deduct? You must withdraw that excess amount (and any interest or other income attributable to it) from the SEP before the date for filing a tax return, otherwise you will be subject to a 6% penalty tax on the excess contribution. Not only will you be assessed a penalty in the year of the overcontribution, but also in subsequent years until that excess is removed. Furthermore, if you remove the excess amount and any interest or income it earned, you will be assessed a 10% tax on the interest or income since that is treated as a premature distribution. (Sometimes, as the saying goes, you can't win for losing.) But look on the bright side. You may be able to apply that excess contribution toward the following year's contribution. These are the same rules that apply for your own IRA (see Chapter 2).

Vesting

You are always fully vested in your SEP-IRA. In other words, you immediately own any amounts contributed to your account by your employer. Therefore, if you change jobs, you take the full amount in your SEP with you.

Investments

Because a SEP is an IRA, we won't repeat our list of SEP investment alternatives here. See Chapter 2 for IRA details and Chapters 7 and 8 for investment strategies.

Employee Withdrawals

Your employer cannot prohibit you from withdrawing funds from your SEP, and you always have unrestricted access to those sums. If you do withdraw any amount, however, you will still be subject to the same 10% premature distribution penalty tax as on an IRA. In general, SEPs are subject to the same tax provisions concerning withdrawals as IRAs.

Depending on the contractual terms of the SEP-IRA to which your employer is contributing, you may be able to move all or part of your funds to another IRA, for instance, if a better return is available. If your SEP does allow this, there are two legal ways to switch your funds to another IRA.

You can use a rollover, whereby you remove the funds from the original account and actually take possession of the money. You have 60 days to use that money before you must deposit it in another IRA or SEP plan. You can only use this provision once a year, and there are penalties if you do not get your money back into an IRA within 60 days.

You may also be able to transfer funds directly between trustees. In this case, you do not take possession of the funds, and thus have no IRS problems if the funds aren't moved within a certain amount of time. You must instruct your current account trustee to send the funds directly to a different IRA. There is no limit to the number of times each year you can transfer funds in this manner. However, be warned that in transferring your IRA, you will be charged various fees on both ends that can add up quickly.

Should you change employers, your employer's SEP contributions are already in your own IRA. Therefore, there is no need to worry about rolling over the funds into another account as is the case with other retirement plans. Of course, you can change your investment ·if you so desire. For further details on rollovers and transfers, see the section on IRAs in Chapter 2.

Tax Treatment at Retirement

The IRA rules (pertaining to tax treatment of distributions and inadequate withdrawals after age 70½) are applicable to your SEP-IRA. Briefly, you may begin withdrawing from your SEP when you are 59½, but you must begin taking distributions by April 1 of the year following the year in which you turn age 70½. There is, however, one exception. You may still take tax deductions for payments made by your employer to your SEP after you are 70½.

If your employer regularly funds a SEP, you are fortunate. All funds contributed belong to your retirement nest egg. What's more, you will not lose any money should you change jobs. Finally, you get to decide how your retirement savings will be invested.

ESOPs

Another type of benefit your employer may offer is an ESOP. Technically known as an Employee Stock Ownership Plan, an ESOP can assume a variety of forms. The basic ESOP is a tax-qualified employee benefit plan which invests in company securities. Employers love ESOPs—they offer a flexible way to finance corporate growth. As far as employees are concerned, the ESOP gives them a "piece of the action" through ownership of company stock.

The typical plan involves some type of stock bonus plan, either on its own, or combined with an optional employee stock purchase plan. The ESOP can also have some of the features common in profit-sharing plans. However, unlike some pension or other retirement plans, the employer doesn't have to make contributions to the ESOP based on profit sharing or a fixed contribution level.

Nonetheless, as with profit-sharing plans, there must be a definite formula for allocating employer contributions among the ESOP plan participants; the ESOP must be a defined contribution plan. The ESOP must also be designed to meet qualification requirements for employee plans as well as specific ESOP rules. Finally, if the ESOP permits voluntary contributions from employees, those funds must be matched by employer contributions that are used to purchase additional shares.

Bread and Butter ESOP

Here's how the typical ESOP is structured. Your employer sets up a plan trust and designates a plan trustee. Your employer can then make tax-deductible cash or stock contributions to the plan. If the contributions are in cash, those contributions are used to purchase company stock. If the stock held in the ESOP has voting rights, then plan participants must receive those voting rights as shares are allocated to their accounts.

In general, the company stock remains in the plan until you retire or otherwise separate from service. At that point, you receive distributions from the plan in the form of stock or in some instances cash. You always have the right, however, to demand that the distribution be in the form of your employer's securities.

Life Insurance Benefits

The IRS has said that, subject to some restrictions, assets of the ESOP may be used to purchase life insurance. One of the restrictions is that the aggregate life insurance premiums allocated to you as a participant must not be greater than 25% of the amount allocated to your ESOP at any particular time. While the primary investment of the ESOP will be your company's stock, you can also receive incidental life insurance benefits. Should you die, proceeds of the life insurance policy would be paid to your beneficiaries so that they receive a cash benefit in addition to stock. In some instances, the employer may structure the life insurance so that the firm is the beneficiary; in this case, the benefits of the policy could be used by the corporation to repurchase your stock.

Distributions

As an ESOP participant, you have the right to require that your ESOP benefits be given to you in the form of the employer's stock. Furthermore, if your employer's stock is not actively traded, you are entitled to a "put option"—you can require the employer to repurchase the stock, according to a written schedule that conforms to fair market values.

Of course, you can get an ESOP distribution when you retire. You can also get a distribution when you quit your job or are laid off or fired before normal retirement age. Unless you make a written request, distribution can be held up for a year after you retire, die, or become disabled, or *five* years after you leave the employer's service for other reasons (e.g., quitting). And read the plan carefully: The plan can provide for distributions over a period of one to five years (even longer, for balances over $500,000).

What can you do with that portion of a lump-sum distribution that is currently taxable? Roll it over into an IRA or apply five-year forward averaging. These options help you avoid regular income tax in the current year.

Moreover, there is a special tax planning strategy you can use only with an ESOP. It may make sense if you're not planning to hold on to the stock you receive. When you get your lump sum, you can subtract the amount of appreciation of your employer's stock *before* you apply five-year averaging rules. Thus, when you sell your shares, you actually get to record the cost basis of the shares and, therefore, will actually pay taxes on an amount that is less than the value you actually received. Of course, this assumes that the stock has appreciated in value while you held it in the ESOP.

Finally, should you decide to sell the stock, you may be required to sell it to your employer first, before you sell it to another party.

Who Offers the ESOP

Generally speaking, only corporations can set up an ESOP plan. Nonprofit organizations, the government, and other nonstock issuing organizations would not be able to provide such a plan.

Pension and Profit-Sharing Plans

Pension Plans

Ever since the company pension plan became a fixture in corporate America, workers have depended on their pensions to provide steady retirement income. Despite the rapid spread of IRAs, for most people, employer-sponsored pension plans will most likely remain a retirement planning cornerstone.

The basic idea is that your employer establishes and maintains a pension plan for you so that you'll have retirement income for a specified period of time, generally, the rest of your life. Note, however, that a pension plan does not provide regular temporary disability income.

As far as your company is concerned, the plan is a fixed obligation —it must be funded whether the business has a good or bad year. The plan's funding is not contingent on the firm's profitability (as is the case with a profit-sharing plan). An overriding benefit to your company is that it gets a current tax deduction for its contributions to the plan. Let's look at the most common types of pension plans.

Defined Contribution

The defined contribution, or money-purchase, plan requires that the employer make fixed annual contributions to your pension account. Although you know how much your company contributes on your behalf each year, the total amount of your account balance at retirement will also include any investment income that the contributions have earned over time. Your employer's fixed annual contribution is usually expressed as a percentage of your salary.

Target Benefit

A target benefit plan aims at providing you with some predetermined "target" benefit, but it does not guarantee that you will receive that amount. After determining the desired benefit assumed for each person, your company calculates how much it needs to contribute on your behalf each year. Included in this calculation are assumptions about the amount of investment income those funds will earn. At retirement, however, the amount you receive will not necessarily be that targeted amount. Rather, the exact amount of your benefit will depend on the value of the assets in the pension pool.

Defined Benefit

The most common—and most familiar—type of pension arrangement is the defined benefit plan. As the name suggests, this type of plan guarantees you a certain benefit when you retire. The actual annual amount you receive is determined according to a specific formula defined by your employer.

The formula is generally based on length of service, compensation, or a combination of the two. You might receive a stated monthly or yearly payment for each month or year of service. Or, your benefit might be based on your average compensation for a stated number of years or your compensation at retirement.

No matter how your benefit is defined, your employer has to fund the plan to ensure that you will receive retirement income. An actuary determines your employer's annual contribution on the basis of age and life expectancy of all employees, employee turnover, and the amount the plan is likely to earn. The goal is to ensure that the pension fund will be large enough to fund each person's retirement benefit.

Profit-Sharing Plans

Profit-sharing plans are actually a type of defined contribution plan. Your employer sets up a profit-sharing plan so that you and other workers share in company profits. A profit-sharing plan is typically set up as an employee trust, and the employer makes contributions according to a stated method, which can be somewhat flexible. One benefit to the employer is that in years of meager profits, the contribution amount can be reduced or even eliminated.

Requirements

To be "tax-qualified" any benefit plan set up by your employer must pass certain legal tests. For one thing, the plan must be described in writing and it must be in effect (not just on the drawing board). The plan must also be permanent and meet legal requirements that govern employee participation and coverage. Moreover, the plan cannot discriminate among employees; it especially cannot favor officers of the firm or employees who are highly compensated or who are shareholders.

Pension and profit-sharing plans have been around for some time, but ERISA and other, more recent legislation—such as the Retirement Equity Act of 1984—established far-reaching guidelines and new regulations for plan sponsors. There are now strict rules concerning eligibility, insurance of benefits, faster vesting, and provisions for automatic joint and survivor benefits.

Employer Contributions

As we explained above, employer contributions to a defined benefit plan are determined by actuarial formulas that concern assumed benefits paid to workers when they retire.

Year in and year out, a profit-sharing plan does not contribute a fixed portion of profits to the plan. But there must be a set formula for allocating benefits among plan participants. As with other defined contribution retirement plans, profit-sharing plans are subject to limitations on employer contributions. The law says that "annual additions" on your behalf cannot exceed $30,000 or 25% of your annual salary, whichever is less. This limitation applies to the aggregate contribution made by your employer to all defined contribution plan accounts established for you.

Note, however, that the amount that may be deducted by an employer contributing to a profit-sharing plan is limited to 15% of the total compensation paid to participating workers during the tax year.

In the case of either plan, contributions made by your employer are not taxable to you when they are made, and earnings on these contributions also accumulate without taxation. In general, you will be taxed when you begin to receive distributions from the plan.

Employee Contributions

A pension plan may require employees to contribute to the plan, but it cannot be structured so that only the highest paid employees can afford to make the minimum contribution. As a rule of thumb, the IRS considers mandatory employee contributions of 6% or less to be acceptable and not burdensome.

Vesting

Your own contributions to the plan are immediately "vested": You have an unqualified right to them. But employers are allowed to set up plans that require employees to work a given length of time before becoming entitled to the amounts the employer contributed to the plan for them. The employer can set its own vesting schedule, provided that the employee is *either* unvested for five years, then 100% vested; or 20% vested after 3 years, 40% after 4 years, 60% after 5 years, 80% after 6 years, and 100% after seven years.

Borrowing

The plan can be written to allow you to borrow against your pension benefits. A loan is not considered a premature distribution, so you don't have to worry about the 10% tax penalty. Under most circumstances, the loan won't be considered taxable income, either.

The exception: loans over $10,000 or half of your accrued plan benefit (but not more than $50,000), whichever is greater. To escape treatment as taxable income, you must be required to repay the loan within five years—unless the purpose of the loan is purchase of your principal residence.

Investing

If your pension plan is a defined contribution plan, or if your employer offers a profit-sharing plan, you have several advantages over an employee with a defined benefit plan. For starters, you will probably get to decide how your account balance will be invested. Instead of just accepting your employer's choice of investment approach, you can structure your investments to suit your own investment personality.

The flip-side of this is having to take responsibility for your own investment decisions. (Believe it or not, some people don't want to make their own choices; they mistakenly believe that successful investing is reserved for wealthy folks with high IQs.) In any case, your employer—who wants to avoid any legal liability—will give you little advice on where to invest or when you should switch your funds among investment vehicles.

Investment choices might include a money market mutual fund, a growth stock mutual fund, a bond fund, company stock (if available), and an annuity. More sophisticated plans may offer a larger variety of mutual funds, real estate, and other investments.

If you are a younger employee, you may want to take on some risk —the trade-off when you're searching for maximum capital appreciation—and invest in an aggressive growth fund. If you are in the middle of your working career, you may want to be a bit more conservative and invest your benefit account in a mutual fund that holds stock in companies that pay regular dividends. Upon approaching retirement, chances are you'll want to have some fixed-income investments. (See Chapters 7 and 8 for more details on investment strategies.)

Benefit Limitations

It should be clear by now, with a defined contribution plan the amount you put in and the earnings it accumulates determine the amount available upon retirement. There are various ways (explained below) to take your money out, either after you retire or if you leave your job.

With a defined benefit plan, however, you will receive payments from your employer according to a set allocation formula. But limits are placed on the amount of "annual benefit" payable by your employer. For example, to receive the maximum allowable annual benefit, you must have been a plan participant for ten years. If you do not meet the ten year test, the maximum you can receive in a year is reduced according to a special calculation that your employee benefits representative will be happy to explain.

At Retirement

When you retire, reach age 59½, are disabled, or leave your job, you are entitled to part, if not all, of your benefits from either your pension or profit-sharing plan. How are these benefits treated for tax purposes? Your retirement plan could offer you several options with different tax implications.

Lump Sum Distributions

A lump sum distribution does not necessarily have to be made in a single payment, as long as it is made in one taxable year. To qualify as a lump sum distribution, the payment must also be the balance due to you from your account (this includes all trusts which are part of the plan). It must be made on account of your death, disability, separation from service, or attaining age 59½, and it must be made from a qualified pension, profit-sharing or stock bonus plan.

If, however, you have reached age 59½ *and* continue to work, you cannot take a lump sum distribution from your *pension* plan. If you are still working when you reach normal retirement age (65), you can take a lump sum distribution even though you continue to work. In contrast, a profit-sharing plan can provide you with a lump sum distribution when you reach 59½, whether or not you continue to work.

Any amounts in the plan which are attributable to deductible employee contributions *are not* considered as part of the lump sum distribution and are not eligible for the related favorable tax treatment. Therefore, these amounts can be distributed in a different tax year or over a number of years without any effect on the lump sum distribution.

When you receive a lump sum distribution, you may receive a portion of it tax-free. That amount is equal to all nondeductible contributions you made to the plan, any contributions your employer made that you were taxed on and repayments of loans that were treated as distributions. (You've already paid ordinary income taxes on these funds.) In addition, if you have any stocks or bonds issued by your employer in the distribution, any net unrealized appreciation is removed from the value of the distribution before determining the tax. What is left after you subtract these amounts out is your "total taxable amount." (Your net unrealized appreciation becomes realized —and therefore taxable—when you sell the securities.)

Your "total taxable amount" may be taxed as part capital gain and part ordinary income. The capital gain portion is dependent on the amount of time you were an active participant in the plan prior to 1974. The rough formula to determine the portion of your lump sum distribution that will be treated as a capital gain is as follows:

$$\frac{\text{Pre-1974 months of active participation in the plan}}{\text{months of participation}} \times \text{Taxable Amount} = \text{Capital Gain Total}$$

For example, if you calculated your "total taxable amount" to be $225,000, and if you had been a plan participant for 108 months before 1974 and a plan participant for a total of 264 months, the capital gain portion of the distribution would be 108/264 ×

$225,000 = $92,045. That portion is taxed at a special 20% capital gains rate.

Death Benefits

Many tax-qualified pension, profit-sharing, and stock bonus plans provide death benefits. This can include life insurance proceeds or the account balance of the employee at his or her death. When the benefit is not from life insurance proceeds, your beneficiary can exclude from income a tax-free death benefit up to a maximum of $5,000.

The death benefit exclusion can involve payments made within one taxable year to your beneficiary that are the proceeds from your tax-qualified pension, profit-sharing, or stock-bonus plan. Your beneficiary can also receive any nondeductible contributions made by you to the plan, any contributions made by your employer that were taxable to you, and any loans you had repaid which were treated as taxable distributions. Any death benefit over the exclusion amount is taxable to your beneficiary, according to lump sum distribution rules.

4 Corporate Retirement Plans in Flux: What Happens to Your Benefits?

In Chapter 3, we described the wonderful retirement benefits you can get from your corporate employer. Of course, the ideal scenario is this: Your employer offers a generous pension plan, with top flight professional money managers caring for your nest egg. Meanwhile, your company prospers mightily, and contributions flow to your profit-sharing account. Finally, any shares of company stock you own grow more valuable year in, year out.

However the phrase "they lived happily ever after" is no more guaranteed in employment than in marriage. Several things could occur to mar the smooth progress of your retirement savings program:

- You could quit your job, or get fired.
- The employer could go out of business, or close down the facility in which you work.
- The company could merge with another company, or be taken over.

First things first. If you quit, you may get to take some benefits with you. Your own contributions are always fully vested, so you can get them back. You also get the vested portion of the employer's contributions. The percentage of vesting depends on how long you worked for the company, and the terms of the plan.

If you get this money because you have completely "separated from service," and if the whole amount is paid within one taxable year (not necessarily the year of separation of service, since you can park the money with your ex-employer for a while), then you can treat the part that derives from work for the employer before 1974 as capital gain. You can also roll the money over into an IRA (escaping current tax but also denying yourself use of the money) or perhaps use five-year forward averaging. You can use five-year forward averaging if you are over age 59½ at the time of the distribution.

You can get capital gain treatment for pre-1974 amounts if the company you worked for is taken over by another company and liquidated. However, if the company is merged or consolidated, but not liquidated, and you continue your old job for the new company, you haven't "separated from service," so you don't get capital gain treatment even if you do receive a lump sum.

Plan Mergers; Company Mergers

It's very possible that, even if the company you work for engages in a merger, your pension plan will continue operations just as before. In other words, just because two companies merge, that doesn't necessarily mean that their pension plans merge.

If there's no plan merger, there won't be any noticeable effect on your pension. However, if the plans do merge, the tax laws and the Department of Labor's pension rules impose what is called the "before and after" rule. Under this rule, the merger of the plans must be done in such a way that, if the plan terminates right after the merger, consolidation, or transfer of plan assets, you will get benefits at least as good as you would have received if the plan had terminated right before the merger, consolidation, or asset transfer. Put another way, your pension money can't be swallowed up in the transfer.

For a defined contribution plan, this works out so that the plan account balance in your name must be at least as great after the change as before. For a defined benefit plan, the measuring instrument is the present value of all your accrued benefits before the change—including benefits that have accrued but are not vested because you haven't been working for the employer long enough.

If one of the plans is a defined benefit plan, and the other plan involved in the merger, consolidation, or asset transfer is a defined contribution plan, one of the plans will have to be changed to conform to the other.

Plan Termination

Theoretically, pension plans must be designed to be "permanent" if they are to be tax-qualified at all, and if the corporation wants to be able to deduct its contributions from its taxable income. But there are certain events that are legally considered valid reasons for terminating a pension plan:

- the employer's bankruptcy or insolvency.
- discontinuance of the business itself for good reason.
- the sale of the business (or a major alteration in its stockholdings) —as long as the transaction is at arm's length, not a "put up job" between related parties.
- financial inability to continue the plan.

When a pension plan is negotiated as part of a union contract, the employer will probably insist on an "escape clause" that allows termination of the plan when one of these events occurs; otherwise, the employer can't change or terminate the plan as long as the union contract remains in force.

A plan can also be partially terminated if coverage is limited or certain employees are excluded from coverage.

Some plan terminations are voluntary (from the employer's point of view—the employees are seldom overjoyed). The Pension Benefit Guaranty Corporation (PBGC), which is part of the Department of Labor, can also force termination of a plan if it has not been funded sufficiently by the employer, isn't being run properly, or otherwise imperils your rights to your benefits.

If a plan is terminated or frozen (that is, the employer stops making contributions), you must be given the option of getting your benefits in the form of joint and survivor annuities, just like any other plan. Whether or not the PBGC is involved, the plan must distribute its assets as fast as it can.

The PBGC

If the plan is a defined contribution plan, then there's a clear mandate: The amounts credited to each plan participant's accounts vest as soon as the plan terminates or partially terminates. The IRS will also make sure that termination is not used as a way to distribute a disproportionate amount of plan assets to top officers or stockholders of the corporation who are close to retirement age when the plan terminates.

A defined benefit plan creates more difficult problems, because the employer does not establish an identifiable account for each employee. A schedule must be followed to allocate the plan's assets among the participants.

First, assets are used to repay employees for their voluntary contributions to the plan. Next, employees get back contributions they were required to make to the plan as a condition of employment and plan participation. Then, benefits to retirees that were in pay status for the three years before termination are allocated. (This class includes payments that would have been payable to employees who were eligible for retirement but chose not to retire.) Next, plan assets are distributed up to the maximum amount insured by the PBGC; then come benefits that have been vested but are not insured by the PBGC; and, finally, other benefits under the plan.

As you can imagine, plans that are about to terminate are likely to run out of money long before this sequence is fully played out. Therefore, the PBGC provides insurance for defined benefit plans. (Insurance for defined contribution plans isn't necessary, because participants can always get the balances in their accounts.)

PBGC's reach

Employers have to pay premiums for the PBGC insurance, and they have an obligation to repay the PBGC for some or all of the insurance proceeds paid out to employees after termination. Over 100,000 defined benefit plans are insured by the PBGC, and about 38 million employees are protected by the PBGC. However, the

PBGC has an uncanny resemblance to the Federal Deposit Insurance Corporation: A few really dramatic plan terminations will put it out of business.

The PBGC does not ensure that participants in terminated defined benefit plans will be as well-off as they would have been if the plan had not terminated. The PBGC won't cover more than the equivalent of a straight life annuity beginning at normal retirement age; nor will it cover more than the actuarial equivalent of $750 a month or 100% of the participant's average wages during the five highest-paid years of employment (whichever is smaller). A warning: Employers "phase in" PBGC coverage. So, if the plan terminates during its first five years, employees will not get full PBGC protection.

Obviously, it pays to know the ins and outs of basic pension plan law. Perhaps you're now being courted by two companies that would give their eye teeth to have you on board. And, perhaps, all else being equal, one offers you better protection against the risks of retirement plan terminations or changes. You'll know what to do.

5 403(b)—The Teachers' Friend or Profits for the Nonprofit Crowd

Employees of nonprofit organizations and public schools usually don't have pension plans, but they too have to save for retirement. Our nation's lawmakers—who never miss a chance to woo voters—decided to allow this special class of workers to take care of themselves. In fact, IRS code 403(b) retirement savings programs were the model for the universal IRA we all now enjoy.

For its part, the IRS has once again demonstrated its uncanny flair for administering tax-advantaged retirement savings programs; the official language describing 403(b) plans is enough to make a CPA chew through a whole box of pencils. Consider this: If you are a common-law employee of a Code 501(c)(3) organization or a public school system (Code 403(b)), you can save for your retirement with a 403(b) or 403(b)(7) plan.

Let's try plain English. If you are employed by a nonprofit organization (within certain limitations that your employer can worry about) or by the public schools, you can save for your retirement with a tax-deferred contribution plan called a 403(b). The name comes from the relevant section of the IRS code.

Two Choices

Code section 403(b) provides that tax-deferred contributions be used to purchase an annuity contract. For a while, only insurance companies were able to offer the plan. However, additions to the original code section—403(b)(7)—now allow investments in closed- or open-end mutual funds.

At present, these are the *only* two types of financial institutions allowed to issue a 403(b) contract. Since your employer chooses the investment options available for your 403(b) plan, your investment choices may seem restricted, compared with an IRA program. Still, many insurers and mutual fund companies offer a good selection of investment options for 403(b) plans. Like the popular 401(k) plan, the monies you contribute are tax-deductible in the current year and all of the earnings are tax-deferred until you begin withdrawals.

That means the 403(b) offers the power of pretax compounding. The money you would have paid in taxes each year on the earnings in the plan is reinvested to your benefit. That, combined with enforced reinvestment of all your earnings over a prolonged period, really makes these fantastic savings vehicles.

Unlike a 401(k), a 403(b) plan does not need IRS approval, and in general, the qualification requirements for a 401(k) are not applicable to the 403(b). In fact, an organization need not meet the strict nondiscrimination provisions of the 401(k). Your employer may discriminate freely between employees (for example, not offer the plan to all employees) and may even cover part-time employees.

Salary Reduction Agreement

There are two ways contributions can be made to your 403(b): Your employer can make a contribution to your plan account with no reduction in your salary or you can have your salary reduced each payday through payroll deduction.

The first is the "addition-to-salary" arrangement. Many tax-exempt organizations, however, are not allowed to make contributions in addition to your salary. In this case, you may make an arrangement to reduce your salary or forgo an expected raise in salary to fund your plan. Under this "salary reduction agreement," your employer will then purchase an annuity for you, or invest in a mutual fund. For tax purposes, the amount contributed to your plan is treated as if it were contributed by the employer and is not taxable to you in the current year.

While it's not required, it's a good idea to document your agreement with your employer carefully in writing, just in case the IRS someday contends that you have, in fact, received that portion of your salary. Always keep in mind that although you are reducing your salary, you are also reducing your taxable income. As a result, you'll pay less in income taxes each year and may in fact slip into a lower tax bracket. The Social Security Administration, however, will consider your 403(b) contributions as part of your earnings base. For this reason, your contributions are subject to FICA. (Prior to 1984, contributions were not considered wages for FICA, but the Social Security Amendments Act of 1983 changed that.)

Limits

Of course, you won't be allowed to fund your 403(b) retirement plan without *any* limits imposed. One qualification requirement that does hold for 403(b) plans is a limit on contributions. And this limit is a bit more complicated to figure out than that for IRAs or 401(k)s. You may exclude from your gross income premiums paid to the 403(b), up to the annual exclusion allowance.

What is the exclusion allowance? Take 20% of your includable compensation (amount earned in the past year excluding annuity payments and nontaxable contributions to a state teacher's retirement fund), multiply that by the number of years of service (years of full-time employment) and then subtract from that product the total amount of 403(b) premiums paid by your employer in past years.

Just as TC '86 sharply reduced the maximum annual employee contribution to 401(k) plans, the new law puts a dollar limit on the amount of salary the employee can elect to defer into a 403(b): $9,500.

The Inevitable Exceptions

As with most rules, there are exceptions to the contributions limits for 403(b) plans. Called catch-up exceptions, they are available to you only if you work for an educational institution, a hospital, home health service agency, welfare agency, or church. The catch-up exception is designed for people who have made small contributions early in their careers. The idea is to allow them to "catch up" by making higher contributions later on.

There are three formulas for determining how to calculate the catch-up exception amount, but suffice it to say that you can only pick one of the methods, and your choice, once made, is irrevocable. Your employer should be able to help you decide.

Save More Than with an IRA

It should be clear at this point that since your contributions are based on a percentage of your salary, you can probably sock away more per year into your 403(b) or 403(b)(7) than into your IRA. Thus, it's only logical to fund your 403(b) plan fully BEFORE you fund your IRA (especially as getting at your money may be easier with the 403(b), which we will discuss below).

Paying the Premiums

If your plan is investing in an annuity, there are two ways the premiums may be paid. First, you can use a single premium annuity contract (the premium is paid with one lump sum); this necessitates a recalculation of your exclusion allowance each year, since you are essentially purchasing a new contract each year.

Second, there is a level annual premium annuity. Most people with steady salaries prefer that their employers establish this type of annuity for them so that the same contribution to the 403(b) plan is made each year. Of course, there are formulas for determining the maximum salary deduction for both types of annuity contracts. One caveat: Any tax-deferred annuity used for a 403(b) cannot have a life insurance provision attached to it.

Overcontributing

What happens if you overcontribute to your 403(b) or 403(b)(7) plan in any given year? You are, not surprisingly, penalized. First, the excess contribution will not be deductible from your salary for income tax purposes. If the excess contribution is used to pay a premium on an annuity contract, you are not further penalized. If, however, that excess has been paid into a custodial account (i.e., a mutual fund) you are also liable for a 6% excise tax on that excess contribution.

Withdrawals

Now that you've been diligently saving for your retirement, what happens if some emergency arises and you need to get at that money? As you could probably guess, conditions and fees to withdraw money vary greatly from one plan to the next. Some plans will allow you to withdraw funds before you reach the age of 59½ without charge, while some will charge a fee or not allow it at all. You will have to pay ordinary income taxes on the withdrawn amount. In addition, some 403(b) annuity plans will allow you to borrow in the case of an emergency.

Loans

Care should be exercised in borrowing, however. In general, when an annuity contract permits a loan, the loan will not be treated as taxable income to the employee—as long as the loan amount, plus the amount of all other loans outstanding, does not exceed $50,000.

In addition, if your loan does not require repayment within five years, then the principal balance is considered a taxable distribution.

Getting your money out of a 403(b)(7) plan offered by a mutual fund can be harder than from an annuity plan offered by an insurance company. The IRS rules on borrowing from a 403(b)(7) are unclear, and some funds simply do not allow borrowing. Most funds will allow you to take distributions for reasons of disability or bona fide financial hardship.

Choosing Plan Investments

As with an IRA or 401(k), the investment vehicle you choose for your 403(b) money depends on the stage you are at in life. For instance, assuming you have a range of investment options to choose from, each with different risk and return characteristics, you should opt for more capital growth if you have most of your working life ahead of you.

The point is that investing for maximum capital appreciation is best achieved when you (1) have the luxury of time on your side and (2) can afford to take a higher risk in pursuit of super returns. Investing in, say, a mutual fund that seeks maximum capital appreciation by buying stocks of fast growth companies often calls for patience and a willingness to take and understand risk. The big payoff may come eventually, but the road to riches may be a bit bumpy at times. If you're just beginning your career, you've got time to shoot for the stars.

On the other hand, if you are close to retirement, you'll want to invest in vehicles such as treasury bills that are "safer" and pay a higher current yield. The idea here is to reduce your investment risk and therefore assure your retirement security. (See Chapters 7 and 8 for an in-depth discussion of investment strategies.)

Switching

Within a 403(b)(7) plan, changing your mind about investment options should be fairly straightforward—as your needs change, switch from one mutual fund in the menu of options to another. Most employers' plans allow you to switch between most or all funds in a particular mutual fund family, though some may restrict you to a select few choices.

On the other hand, with annuities, the transfer can be more complicated. In either case, your employer may well impose limits on the amount, frequency of switches or even set specific times each year that you can transfer.

There are three basic ways for you to switch from one annuity plan to another, or, if available, to a mutual fund. Overall, be sure that the transfer is properly structured so that you avoid any tax liability. (The IRS has not issued a definitive ruling on switching from a mutual fund into an annuity. It seems to love to make it more difficult.)

Your first option is to exchange one annuity contract for another plan through your employer. First, you make a binding agreement with your employer, and then immediately turn over the proceeds of the surrendered contract to your employer. The employer, in accordance with the binding contract, then immediately invests the proceeds into another annuity contract or mutual fund, if provided.

"Help!" you say. "My employer refuses to get involved in a transfer. What do I do?" Don't panic. The IRS decided that an employee can directly surrender one 403(b) annuity for another (or a mutual fund). In this case, you must enter a binding contract with the new plan trustee.

That new organization agrees to accept and invest your funds in an annuity or mutual fund that satisfies 403(b) requirements. Before you surrender your original contract, you should also enter into a binding contract with the original issuer that obligates you to reinvest the proceeds of your surrendered policy into a new annuity contract. And, to be on the safe side, you should "restrictively" endorse the check from your old policy so that it can be used only for the purchase of the new contract. If it can be arranged, however, the preferred way to transfer funds would be directly from your first custodian to the new one (that is, you never touch the check or the funds). DO IT CAREFULLY—DOCUMENTATION IS ESSENTIAL. As you can see, this method can be very complicated.

Rolling Over into an IRA

The last method of exchanging coverage involves rolling over the proceeds, or a part of the proceeds of your plan, into your IRA (individual retirement annuity or account). This involves legal considerations that are different from the transactions explained above;

those were essentially "like-kind" exchanges—from one 403(b) plan to another.

You can make a tax-free rollover of a distribution from your 403(b) plan into an IRA only when the distribution qualifies as a "lump-sum" distribution, or a partial distribution. In other words, if you have (1) reached age 59½, (2) left your employer's service or (3) become disabled, you can take out the balance remaining in your plan, and roll it over to your IRA.

You do, however, have to transfer that amount into your IRA within 60 days in order to qualify for the tax-deferred treatment of rollovers. If you are rolling over assets other than cash, then the identical property must be transferred into the IRA.

A Few More Rules

Before you attempt this IRA rollover method, you should remember that any distribution made should not be arbitrary—i.e., if you are still working and contributions are being made to your 403(b) plan, you cannot normally instruct your employer/plan to make a distribution.

Secondly, keep in mind that if you withdraw money from the IRA prior to age 59½, you will be assessed a 10% penalty tax for premature distribution. (See Chapter 2 for details about IRA rollovers.) That 10% penalty is not applicable in the 403(b)—either the original plan or one you could have exchanged into using the first two methods. Therefore, don't try to use an IRA rollover as a ruse to get at your money. Rather, just take it out and pay ordinary income tax on it.

Taxation

Now, for our favorite subject, taxes. As discussed above, if you surrender your policy by leaving your job, becoming disabled, or attaining age 59½ but remaining employed, then, as long as you follow the above procedures for transferring coverage, you will not be taxed. But, if you surrender your annuity contract, and do not use one of those tax-free exchanges, you will be taxed.

At Retirement

When you retire and begin receiving income from your plan, you will generally report that income in the year in which it is received. If, however, you reported as taxable income a portion of your employer's contributions, then to the extent reported, a portion of your retirement income is tax-free.

It should be noted that distributions from your 403(b) or 403(b)(7) plan, if made in a lump sum, are not eligible for the lump-sum tax treatment—i.e., five-year forward averaging.

Like 401(k)s, 403(b) plans can be a very advantageous way to save for your retirement years. As with all other plans, you have to play within the IRS rules to avoid being penalized and save the most you can for your retirement years.

6   Tools for the Self-Employed: This Could Be You

Once in a while, a politician does something great and earns a place in history. Eugene Keogh, the former New York Congressman, did just that in the early 1960s when he sponsored the legislation that produced—you guessed it—Keogh plans. Although the early version of the Keogh was crippled by severe participation and contribution rules, the modern Keogh, also known as an HR-10 plan, gives self-employed workers the retirement savings punch that their corporate counterparts have come to know and love.

If you earn income from self-employment—even if you work full-time for someone else—the Keogh plan is a good way to build a substantial retirement fund while saving on taxes. Through a Keogh, you save for retirement with annual plan contributions that are deductible from your federal tax bill. What's more, your annual Keogh contributions and any investment income earned remain tax-free until withdrawn when you retire after age 59½.

It's tax-deferred compounding that makes Keoghs and other so-called "tax-qualified" retirement plans so irresistible. When you make steady annual contributions and achieve a reasonable rate of return, your investment profits are reinvested free from current federal taxes and, in turn, earn more money.

Who Can Have a Keogh?

The common denominator is that you earn income from being self-employed. Not only can doctors and lawyers set up Keoghs, but also free-lance writers, computer repairmen, house painters, barbers, and anyone else who earns money from an unincorporated business. Even Uncle Charley, who sells antique bottle caps at the local flea markets, can set up a Keogh.

What about the people you employ? Sure, they can have Keoghs —in fact, the law says that if you are a self-employed person, and you set up your own Keogh, you must extend its benefits to your workers. We'll go into more detail on employee Keoghs below. For now, we'll concentrate on Keoghs established by owner-employees. These are people who own more than 10% of, or derive more than 10% of the profits from, the business.

Keogh vs. IRA

A Keogh plan is like an IRA in that you set up an account or related arrangement and make tax deductible contributions. And, like IRA earnings, any investment profit is tax-free until you begin to draw on it. Finally, a Keogh is like an IRA in that you may begin to withdraw funds from your account when you retire at age 59½ and must begin to withdraw by age 70½. When you reach 70½, however, you'll see how IRA and Keogh age rules differ: You may contribute to a Keogh as long as you are earning income from self-employment, even after 70½. In contrast, you cannot make contributions to your own IRA after 70½ (although you can contribute to a spousal IRA for a mate who is under 70½ and has no earnings).

When it comes to getting the most mileage out of tax-deferred savings power, there is no real contest. The Keogh wins hands down. Unlike an IRA, you can accumulate far more than $2,000 a year in your Keogh. Generally speaking, you can contribute annually up to $30,000, or 20% of your net self-employment profits, whichever is less. (Theoretically, you can contribute up to 25% of net earned income, but the 25% figure is misleading. Because of the way current tax law defines "earned income," you must subtract the amount you plan to put in your Keogh to arrive at the number on which you base your maximum annual contribution. In effect, you can contribute a maximum of 20% of net profits or $30,000, which-ever is less.)

Keogh Plan Options

The rules on Keogh contribution limits get even stickier when you consider the various types of Keogh programs available. Let's look at four types of Keogh plans and the rules for each. You'll see that getting the most horsepower out of your Keogh depends on which route you go. For example, one type of plan lets you contribute up to 20% of net profits, while another plan has an effective contribution ceiling of 13.04%.

If you start to feel a bit overwhelmed, just remember that when it comes time to sign on the dotted line, the financial institution you choose will probably bend over backwards to help you with the fine print. After all, they're just itching for the chance to manage your Keogh assets.

1. Profit Sharing Keogh. This alternative allows variable annual con-tributions ranging from 0% to 13.04% of net profits (which is equivalent to 0%–15% of net earned income) up to $30,000. If your business has fluctuating profits, this choice allows you to change the percentage you contribute each year. Flexibility is the key: You get to decide how much, how often. The law does not force you to contribute each year to the plan. And, only when you contribute to your own Keogh do you have to contribute the same percentage of eligible earnings for any employees who are plan participants.
2. Money Purchase Keogh. With this option, you can save more each year than you can save with a profit sharing Keogh. Here, you designate a fixed percentage of your income that you will contrib-ute each and every year. The allowed range is 0%–20% of net profits (which is equivalent to 0%–25% of net earned income) up to $30,000. You can increase the fixed percentage, but you can

never decrease it. And, you must contribute this fixed percentage for every participating employee each year, whether or not your business realizes a profit or loss.

3. Paired Option. A paired plan is really a combination of the profit sharing and money purchase options. It's for people who want to contribute more than the maximum 13.04% of net profits permitted by the profit sharing plan alone. You commit to making a fixed annual contribution, for example, 8% of net profits, to the money purchase plan. You can then vary your contribution to the profit sharing plan from 0%–12% of net profits each year at your discretion. By pairing the two plans, you're able to contribute the maximum 20% of net profits (which is equivalent to 25% of net earned income) up to $30,000 any year and still have the flexibility to vary contributions.

These three Keogh plan alternatives fall under the legal category known as defined contribution plans. As you might have guessed, defined contribution plans get their name from the fact that specified annual contributions to a retirement account, and any investment profits they earn, determine the value of the eventual retirement benefit. Defined contribution Keoghs are by far the most popular; they are the simplest and cheapest to set up and administer. The final Keogh option we'll discuss, the defined benefit plan, is a horse of a different color.

4. Defined Benefit Keogh. If you're willing to go to a little more trouble—and spend more money on administration—you can shelter even more of your income from current taxes by using a defined benefit Keogh. In a nutshell, a defined benefit Keogh establishes a monthly retirement benefit, and before you retire you contribute the amount that will fund that benefit, based on certain actuarial assumptions and certain assumptions required by the IRS.

Your eventual retirement benefit is expressed as an annual payout determined by a set allocation formula. You'll have to get an actuary to figure out how much you'll need to contribute each year to get the most beneficial payout when you retire after age 65. If you retire before age 65, the maximum benefit you can receive is reduced according to another set formula.

Furthermore, in years after 1988, the maximum benefit amount will be adjusted for increases in the cost of living. As you can imagine, you'd have to contribute a tremendous amount to fund a $40,000- or $50,000-a-year retirement benefit—especially if you don't have too many years to accumulate the funds. Thus, defined benefit Keoghs are especially attractive for very prosperous self-employed persons who are within about 15 years of retirement age. The perfect candidate is someone over 45 years old earning more than $100,000 annually. If you fit the bill, this plan option will help you sock away plenty of money to guarantee a comfortable retirement.

These plan descriptions will give you a head start on deciding which type of Keogh is right for you. As you read on, you'll get acquainted with the rules on mandatory distribution dates, employee Keoghs and the like. However, before you take the plunge, you'll want to look over brochures from several types of Keogh plan providers. You'll also want to talk things over with your accountant or tax adviser. At some point, you'll have to bite the bullet and decide how you want to invest your Keogh money—through a bank, mutual fund, insurance company or stock broker. (See Chapters 7 and 8 for a comparison of investment alternatives.) This is one of the most important choices you'll have to make.

Keoghs Custom-Fit

Okay. You're convinced that Keoghs are just nifty. But, if you salt away most of your salary, what are you going to live on? Maybe your spouse earns enough money to support the household, or maybe you have lots of investment income. Perhaps you can live on the salary from your regular job, moonlight, and contribute 20% of your self-employment income to a defined contribution Keogh, or even more to a defined benefit Keogh. The key here is that you can have a Keogh plan if you have any self-employment income, even if you have a full-time job working for someone else.

The new tax law stipulates that you can have an IRA in addition to your Keogh—but if you earn too much money annually, you won't be able to take a tax deduction for the amount of your annual IRA contribution. That is, the maximum IRA contribution deduction is allowed for someone with an adjusted gross income under $25,000 a year, and a married couple filing a joint return with an adjusted gross income under $40,000 a year. Married people who file separate returns *never* qualify for the full $2,000 IRA deduction. Moreover, the deduction is phased out completely (with a dollar of deduction lost for every five dollars of income) until single taxpayers with AGI over $35,000 and married joint filers with AGI over $50,000 lose the IRA deduction entirely.

More Eligibility Rules

The Keogh bonanza is not for everyone. First of all, it's limited to sole proprietors and partners, not stockholder-employees of corporations. (If you're a stockholder-employee, and the corporation can't afford a full-dress pension plan, you can have an IRA for yourself or a SEP for yourself and your employees. See Chapter 3.)

Next, a partner who does not have a controlling interest in his or her partnership can't set up a Keogh plan without the agreement of at least a voting majority of the partners, although the other partners don't have to participate in the plan.

Employee Keoghs

Finally, if a Keogh plan covers you as owner of the business, it must also cover employees who are twenty-one years old or who have worked for the business for three years. You can't exclude

contributions to your own Keogh account from taxable income unless appropriate contributions are made to the employees' accounts.
(Oh, well, the contributions to the employees' accounts are deductible as business expenses, but it can still be painful to make them.)
The lesson: Talk to your accountant before you set up a Keogh plan
for yourself if you have employees or think you might in the fore-
seeable future.

Legal Hoops You Must Jump Through

Technically speaking, there are three ways to set up a Keogh plan:
(1) as a trust (it's okay if the owner-employee is the trustee); (2) as
a straight or variable rate nontransferable annuity contract bought
from a life insurance company; and (3) as a "custodial account" set
up with a bank, mutual fund company or similar institution.

A new and very annoying requirement: As of 1985, one-person
Keogh plans, like larger Keogh plans covering a number of employees, must make annual reports to the IRS. The initial report, and
the report for every third year after that, must be made on the IRS
five-page Form 5500-C. In the following two years, the annual report
can be made on the shorter form 5500-R. The 5500-C is more of a
nuisance than anything else—owner-employees may need help from
an accountant or financial institution to cope with the language of the
form, which was really written for larger plans. In fact, many mutual
funds competing fiercely for Keogh accounts will go out of their way
to help you with all the paperwork.

No matter what: Don't ignore the filing requirement. The IRS can
impose a fine of $25 for each day after the July 31 annual deadline
that the form is unfiled or filed but incomplete. The maximum fine
is $15,000 per Keogh account, but don't press your luck. If you're
hopelessly confused, you can get a 2½ month filing extension by
using Form 5558. The one ray of hope in the situation is that the
Form 5500-C is strictly an informational return—you have to disclose
information about your Keogh plan, but you don't have to pay any
taxes at the time you file the 5500-C.

Keogh Investments

If the Keogh is set up as a trust, and the owner-employee is not the trustee, he or she can still give investment instructions to the trustee. The trustee can invest in pretty much anything except collectibles.

Like any retirement savings plan, a Keogh should be invested safely because it will be a critical source of income later in life when you don't have the flexibility to generate new financial resources easily. However, if you have many years to go before retirement, and you expect to retire with income in addition to your Keogh, you can focus on the long term and invest in high-growth investment vehicles such as stock mutual funds that carry some measure of investment risk.

How much risk is appropriate? It depends on a number of factors, including your total financial picture, age, prospects for steady income, long-term liabilities, and investment savvy. We'll take an in-depth look at investment strategies for retirement savings in Chapters 7 and 8. As we'll see, the key to a financially secure retirement is selecting a proper level of investment risk, balancing that risk with potential returns, and executing an intelligent plan that produces a well-diversified portfolio.

We'll see that a number of investment options make sense for Keogh plans. Of course, there's a wide range of mutual funds you might consider—the risk spectrum runs from the very conservative money market funds, to the somewhat risky growth/income stock funds, to the highly speculative growth stock funds. Then there are the Keogh options available from stockbrokers, savings and loans, and banks. The route you choose may depend on whether or not you consider yourself an active investor—if you're willing to keep an eye on your Keogh's investment performance, and if you'll take the time and energy to move assets among investment vehicles in search of maximum capital growth, then you're an active investor. In that case, aggressive growth mutual funds may be right for you. On the other hand, if you prefer to remain a passive investor, you won't mind handing your financial fate over to banks and insurance companies whose investment vehicles typically require little investor brain power.

A Few Yellow Lights

Prohibited Transactions

Some things you might want to do are forbidden as "prohibited transactions" between an owner-employee and his or her Keogh trust. There's a 5% excise tax on these prohibited transactions, and the IRS can impose a 100% penalty if the transaction isn't reversed after the IRS identifies it as prohibited.

For starters, the owner-employee is not allowed to borrow from the trust. This is the one remaining significant difference between the benefits available to the owner of an unincorporated business with a Keogh plan and those perks available to the stockholder-employee of a corporation with a qualified plan—the stockholder-employee can borrow from his or her pension account. (However, an employee who has no financial interest in the business can take loans or hardship withdrawals from a Keogh provided the loan guidelines are uniform.) Moreover, the owner-employee cannot buy property from, or sell property to, the trust, or charge the trust a fee for services rendered —for instance, services as a trustee.

Keogh Plan Withdrawals

The owner-employee can retire at age 59½ and start taking money out of the Keogh account without penalties. Remember, the maximum defined benefit is adjusted for early retirement; and there's an additional 10% income tax penalty on anyone who owns 5% or more of an unincorporated business and draws benefits from its Keogh plan before reaching the age of 59½, unless he or she is disabled.

The owner-employee must begin receiving Keogh benefits by April 1 of the year he or she reaches the age of 70½, even if he or she is still working, otherwise the IRS can claim that the Keogh plan was never qualified to defer tax on compensation—and that means a heap of trouble. However, if the owner-employee is still working after 70½, he or she can still make contributions to the Keogh, concurrent with distributions.

Keogh participants have two basic withdrawal choices: They can either take the total in their account as a lump sum, or they can arrange for a payout over time. Four schemes of periodic payments are acceptable to the IRS:

- payments for the life of the participant.
- payments for the life of the participant and another beneficiary (say, the participant's spouse).
- payments for a certain number of years—provided that the number of years is not longer than the participant's life expectancy.
- payments for a certain number of years—provided that the number of years is not longer than the life expectancy of the participant or his or her beneficiary, whoever can be expected to live longer.

Keogh plans are covered by the Retirement Equity Act (see Chapter 9), so participants must be offered the option of joint and survivor annuities with their spouses. Keogh participants must also have the written consent of their spouses to surrender this option.

Remember, the larger the number of expected payments, the smaller each payment will be. In a typical case, the participant will be a male worker married to a woman younger than he is. If the payments are made over both their lifetimes, or over a number of years measured by her lifetime, there will probably be more but smaller payments than if payments stopped with his death.

What if the participant chooses a payout over a certain number of years, and dies while payments are still being made? In that case, the remaining funds must be distributed at least as quickly as they would have been if the participant remained alive for the full time—the participant's beneficiary can choose to speed up the payments, or receive the remaining funds in a lump sum.

The Taxman Cometh

The general rule is that a lump sum taken from a Keogh account is ordinary income in the year it's received. You can imagine how much fun it is to have an extra $50,000 or even $750,000 in taxable income in the year you retire. Lots of laughs.

Pre-1974 Contributions

Any amount that can be allocated to a Keogh plan contribution made before 1974 is treated as a long-term capital gain. How do you know what is what? The institution paying out the lump sum makes the necessary allocations on the Form 1099R furnished to the recipient of the lump sum. Of course, the IRS also gets a copy.

Rollover to an IRA

One strategy for postponing current taxes after retirement is to roll over at least 50% of your lump sum Keogh distribution to an IRA within 60 days of receipt. To do this, you must make a special election, and the distribution must really be a lump sum, not one in a series of periodic payments. But the amount you retain and do not roll over is taxed as ordinary income in the year you get it; none of it can be treated as a capital gain, and none of it qualifies for forward averaging (we'll get to that in the next paragraph). Of course, you'll eventually have to follow the IRA distribution rules; and an IRA that contains any funds rolled over from any Keogh plan can never be rolled over into a qualified plan.

Another strategy is to use five-year forward averaging. (The old tax code allowed ten-year forward averaging.) With five-year forward averaging, the entire lump sum is taxed as if you withdrew it for five years, one-fifth at a time. There is a bonanza in TC '86 for folks who were at least fifty years old on January 1, 1986. First of all, they can still use ten-year forward averaging, paying taxes in the year of distribution as if the money had been received over a ten-year period. The trade-off is that five-year forward averaging applies the lower TC '86 rates; ten-year averaging applies the older, higher rates.

Remember, no matter how high the pension income you receive, your Social Security benefits will not be reduced (although they probably will be reduced if you earn income by working after your official retirement). However, if your income of all kinds exceeds certain limits (see Chapter 1), part of your Social Security benefits will be treated as taxable income. So do some analysis, or check with your accountant before you choose a payout method for your Keogh plan. Don't take action before you assess its potential tax consequences.

Switching Among Keogh Accounts

In its wisdom, the IRS realizes that you may want to switch your Keogh assets from one fund to another in search of stronger investment performance. Thank you, IRS. But there are a few pitfalls to avoid. Your switch is tax-free as long as the money goes directly from one account to another—if you put your hands on the dough, you're in trouble with the revenuers. Read: reportable income on both principal and earnings and a nondeductible 10% penalty. If you want to switch, instruct your present service provider to send the check directly to the new fund.

In summary, the modern Keogh plan lets the self-employed person save for retirement using the fantastic power of tax-advantaged investing. Sure, the rules are a bit cumbersome. But with a little concentration, and the nerve to ask the right questions, you too can make your retirement years financially sound. If you want to know how the IRS describes Keogh rules, call your regional IRS office and ask for "Tax Information on Self-Employed Retirement Plans" *(Publication 560)*.

7 Debunking Common Investment Myths

Perhaps the two most important decisions you will ever make in your lifetime are (1) where to invest your retirement savings and (2) how to manage your retirement savings.

You can accept the conventional wisdom about where and how to invest—that is, you can trust others to make your decisions for you. Or you can take charge of your retirement nest egg and manage the important moves yourself. Let's take a look at your alternatives.

Common Myths

The conventional wisdom says, "trust me." It is promulgated by salesmen who want you to buy their version of the best deal (read: that which makes the highest commission for them). Once you're sold, they move on. The conventional wisdom is designed to minimize your involvement and "protect" you from making a choice that does not benefit the salesman. We think you ought to decide for yourself what is the best potentially profitable move.

A Correct Fit

The conventional wisdom regarding retirement investing makes several assumptions, some of which may not be right for you. They are as follows:

- This is your retirement nest egg; why take any risks?
- Make your decision for the long-term and forget about it. In other words, solve all your financial problems in the next few minutes.

- Choose the safest investments, those that pay sure dividends and interest.
- This is your retirement money; invest it only in insured investments. You need all of the protection you can get.
- Trust me, I will do it all for you. Turn over the management of your money to us, and we will protect it for your golden years (for an exorbitant fee). Don't worry. Relax and enjoy your retirement.

Try Our Approach

The Donoghue wisdom is an alternative philosophy. Its motto is "Trust yourself." Retirement savings plans offer the investment opportunities of a lifetime. Why waste them? The Donoghue wisdom suggests a proactive approach—it urges you to manage your own retirement money and make your moves according to an informed view of the financial markets. Moreover, the Donoghue wisdom urges you to go all out on your investments. After all, if this is your best chance to build up your retirement nest egg, why not try to make it grow as much as you can?

The Donoghue wisdom urges you to learn how to accept and manage risks, sort of like looking both ways before you cross a busy street. The Donoghue wisdom also says that you should avoid unnecessary service charges and commissions. We also urge you to think big. For example, by investing only $10 a week and managing it so it earns 20% or more a year for 30 years, and doing that through your IRA—deductibility of contributions is a plus, but only a plus— you could be a millionaire.

Gifts for Your Children

There are two important gifts you can give your children: first, the knowledge of how to earn 20% or more a year (we'll explain how in Chapter 8), and, second, some money with which to do it.

Here's an example. If you gave a child $2,000 a year for five years between the ages of 20 and 25, and he or she could learn how to invest that in an IRA at 20% a year until age 65, the result could be over $26 million before taxes at age 65. The power of compounding that money for 40–45 years is so powerful that the $10,000 you gave them would be worth more than the $2,000 a year that they contributed the next 40 years. The bonus of $26 million is for helping them fund their IRAs when they could not afford to do so.

That's the power of the Donoghue wisdom. Trust yourself and you can do better and become financially independent. Trust others, and you will be beholden to them all your life, and they may well let you down.

A Directory of Investment Options

Insured Bank and Thrift Products

Passbook Savings Accounts

Passbook savings accounts are the garden variety savings accounts to which we were all introduced as children. They are available in any amount (although most banks now have minimums below which you get no interest and are "service charged" relentlessly). Moreover, they pay whatever the bank is willing to pay (many banks have lowered their returns below the old 5.5% maximum since it was repealed on April Fool's Day, 1986).

The Conventional Wisdom: At least these are insured, and you have easy access to your money. After all, isn't this just a parking place for your funds until you make that decision to move your money into a conventional CD?

The Donoghue Wisdom: Make your decision to do something with this money NOW or you will end up with very meager retirement pickings. All the insurance is doing is lulling you into not making a decision—or a decent return.

The Bottom Line: Treat yourself well, get your money out of passbook savings accounts, and into something that offers a better return.

Money Market Deposit Accounts (MMDAs)

These are highly popular for insured savings programs of all kinds. They may be established in any amount; however, most banks have their own minimum balance requirements. They can pay competitive money market returns, although few banks choose to oblige you with such returns.

The Conventional Wisdom: They are "just like" money market mutual funds except they are insured. MMDAs pay money market rates on very liquid accounts, providing easy and convenient access.

The Donoghue Wisdom: Actually, they *are* a lot like money funds except they pay less, have more restrictions on their use, and have fees and charges for services money funds offer for free. In addition, your money is still in a bank where the only alternatives for shifting money into the stock market are discount brokerage services and mutual funds that aren't even run by the banks themselves.

The Bottom Line: You can do better. Think longer term and use CDs if you must stay with a bank.

Certificates of Deposit (CDs)

Certificates of deposit are simply savings accounts which promise you a fixed rate of return (or one which varies with, say, Treasury bill rates) if you are willing to tie up your money for a set period of time. They are insured by the federal government and are easy to buy from your local bank.

The Conventional Wisdom: The fixed rate of return allows you to project exactly how much you will earn. What's more, your money is insured up to $100,000 (per depositor, per bank) by the federal government.

The Donoghue Wisdom: It pays to shop nationally for the best deals among federally-insured bank and thrift CDs. They are all equally safe, and you might as well invest with the bank offering the most attractive returns.

The Bottom Line: CDs are worth considering if you shop nationally, but if you have the confidence to invest, why limit your horizons? Buy CDs only when interest rates are high. (See Chapter 8.) Wait out low interest rates in a money fund, where you can sell out at any time without penalty, or for the more adventurous, a stock growth fund.

Pay Attention

If you are truly committed to your retirement savings program, you must fully grasp two things: (1) you may someday have much more than $100,000 in your IRA; and, (2) banks fail. Do not leave uninsured dollars in your bank IRA—that is a serious risk in today's environment. Heads up, folks, this is a time to invest with your eyes wide open.

Mutual Funds

Money Market Mutual Funds

These convenient and highly liquid investments have really become the standard for honest money market returns and excellent customer service. Money funds earn their returns by lending money, short-term, to the federal government and to the largest and safest banks and corporations in the country. They invest in money market instruments such as Treasury bills, repurchase agreements, large bank CDs, commercial paper and similar safe investments. Their safety record is impeccable (bank customers have lost money in the past, whereas money fund shareholders have never lost any money).

The Conventional Wisdom: Money funds are safe, convenient and pay a competitive money fund rate. They make investing for an IRA easy, with low minimum initial requirements. In recent years, they have provided good yields—a real "no-think" investment alternative.

The Donoghue Wisdom: For your retirement savings plan, a money fund account is your "home base." It is where you can wait out the interim between major stock market moves. It's an easy place to start —especially if you pick a money fund in a no-load mutual fund family which becomes the trustee for your IRA. Fund families give you the "run of the house"; you have access to most of the funds in the family. That's important when you become a more confident investor; you'll want to try your hand at moving money in sync with the markets.

The Bottom Line: Money funds are an attractive building block for a sound investment strategy.

Stock Market Mutual Funds

Like money market funds, stock market mutual funds pool money from many investors and invest it in a diversified basket of securities. In the case of stock funds, those securities are primarily equities. These funds are heavily regulated by the Securities and Exchange Commission, and provide investors with professional investment management, diversification and easy purchase and sale.

Stock market and other mutual funds are sold in two basic ways: load and no-load mutual funds. Load mutual funds (a fund is either load or no-load) are sold by brokers who extract a sales charge as high as 8½% from your money. No-load funds eliminate the middle man and have no such sales charge. However, there are also low-load mutual funds that have minimal sales charges (1 to 3%) that may be worth a gander.

The Conventional Wisdom: Here you get two contrasting views. Either (1) you should not invest your retirement money in something as risky as a stock market fund (you can't deduct the losses) or (2) if you really want your retirement money to grow, then you should invest in an aggressive growth mutual fund.

The Donoghue Wisdom: There is only one attitude that is relevant to your IRA or retirement savings plan: More is better than less. It doesn't make any difference how the money is earned (dividends, interest, capital gains). When withdrawn, it is all taxed as ordinary income. (Unless you are allowed to use neat tax advantages like five-year or ten-year forward averaging, you will have to pay regular income taxes on plan withdrawals.) Thank God and Congress they have cut the rates.

There are few places where earning money on your IRA or retirement savings program is easier than in a fund family with no-load funds. The exchange of stock market fund shares for money fund shares can be done over the phone; you don't have to change trustees, and you have the best of all worlds.

The Bottom Line: A stock market mutual fund may be just the ticket for rounding out that sound investment strategy we mentioned before.

Insurance Company Products

Guaranteed Investment Contracts (GICs)

Similar to bank CDs, these are fixed income investments with a specified interest rate and date of maturity. Offered by insurance companies, they are common investment vehicles selected for 401(k) programs. There are often only a few times a year when you can add to or deduct from the contract, although it could very well be once a year.

The Conventional Wisdom: The rate of return is guaranteed (with a set maturity) by an insurance company which "insures" the principal. The rate is sometimes higher than bank CD rates. It's a safe bet.

The Donoghue Wisdom: These convenient and often irrevocable decisions tend to reduce your flexibility to take advantage of opportunities in other markets. You have to wait to get at your money, and you run the risk of being locked in when you should be striving for stock market profits. The dangerous temptation is to leave your money in the "insured" GIC, which you may perceive as the safest alternative.

The Bottom Line: Think hard before locking up your money.

Company Stock

Another favorite for company retirement savings plans, company stock is often used as a way to help employees develop a sense of community with the company. It allows a company to sell or give its stock in lieu of other benefits to many employees who would be unlikely to buy the stock. Sometimes it works. Sometimes it doesn't. Sometimes, whether or not it works as an incentive for employees, the stock takes a nose dive.

The Conventional Wisdom: If the company gives you company stock at a discount, take it and hold onto it. All stocks go up eventually, don't they?

The Donoghue Wisdom: If you can buy company stock at a discount, and you feel it will be a good investment compared to other choices available, take advantage of it. Of course, being on the "inside," you may have a good handle on whether or not your company's stock represents a wise choice.

The Bottom Line: Considering the alternatives, would you choose your company's stock as the primary investment upon which you'll depend for your retirement?

Stockbroker Distributed Products

Zero-coupon Bonds and Similar Products

Zero-coupon bonds, and the like, are highly popular products that have come to the fore in the past few years. You don't buy them in even amounts (for example, $10,000 at a time); rather you buy them at a deep discount (you buy one for, say, $350 to pay off at $10,000 at a specific time).

The Conventional Wisdom: The special feature of these bonds—sometimes called "phantom interest"—is that while you don't receive interest until maturity, outside of an IRA, you would be liable for taxes as though you received the actual interest. Because you're holding it within an IRA (or a similar tax-sheltered retirement plan) you pay no current taxes. Therefore, zeros are ideally suited for your IRA.

The Donoghue Wisdom: The problem with zeros is what they don't tell you: how thin the secondary (resale) market is and what the hidden commissions and fees really are. You could be in for a nasty surprise should you sell before maturity and sell in a rising interest rate environment.

The Bottom Line: If you must buy zeros (or similar products) wait until interest rates have risen substantially and buy them at a significant discount. The point is that you should not be buying any long-term bonds at the bottom of an interest rate cycle.

The Final Word

What about other products sold by stockbrokers? We have only two things to say on this: (1) you don't need to pay commissions to stockbrokers and (2) unless you're very savvy, you're better off investing through mutual funds than buying securities directly.

Appendix A lists mutual fund families tracked over the years by the Donoghue SLYC system (Safety, Liquidity, Yield, and Catastrophe-proofing). These fund families were chosen according to their service features, size, and record for sound management. (These are not necessarily the funds that carry current "buy" recommendations in Donoghue's *MONEYLETTER* ®. See Chapter 8.)

The Donoghue wisdom on saving extends beyond conventional retirement savings plans. You should, of course, be keeping a portion of your savings outside the normal retirement plans. Why? Because you may well need to save for preretirement purchases like a new home, a child's education, a vacation, and the like.

Let's take a look at several investment alternatives we think will be profitable for you. (Retirement savings strategies are covered in Chapter 8.)

Deferred Variable Annuity Plans

These offer the most exciting way to tax-defer the income on after-tax money today. The advantages over normal retirement plans are that you can (1) tax-shelter unlimited amounts of money, (2) have some degree of liquidity through borrowing provisions, (3) borrow part of your money back cheaply, and (4) invest the assets of the annuity in mutual funds and enjoy taking charge of the decisions about which funds offer maximum potential rewards.

(For a free Special Report on Investing in Tax-deferred Annuities in 1987 and Beyond, write to The Donoghue Organization, Box 540, Holliston, Massachusetts 01746.)

Tax-Free Investing

The market timing aspects of The Donoghue Strategy (explained in Chapter 8) can be applied to investing in tax-free money market and bond mutual funds. Post–tax-reform, tax-free yields are expected to become very attractive, especially to those in the 28% and 33% tax brackets.

Taxable Growth Strategies

While we hate paying taxes as much as the next guy, we will pay the piper when mutual fund investments return more than 20% annually. At least the fact that there are no taxes on capital gains until the shares are sold allows us to defer income into later and later tax years.

8 Investment Strategies for Retirement Savings Plans

Kneading the Dough You're Gonna Need

Building your retirement savings is like baking bread. You have to select the right ingredients, follow the recipe, knead the dough a bit, and carefully control the cooking process. The bread we are talking about—the key to your retirement comfort—is worth baking with care.

Unfortunately, too many people miss the meal of a lifetime. They don't take time to select the right ingredients; even worse, they leave the baking to someone else—usually a hungry banker, insurance agent, or stockbroker. The point is that salespeople eat up most of the good stuff at your expense.

Don't Count on Pension Managers

In Chapter 2 we warned you about the danger of relying solely on Social Security for your retirement security. Too many people, whether they're working or retired, also rely heavily on pension fund managers to deliver investment returns high enough to outpace inflation and taxes and to provide a steady retirement income. The sad fact is that pension fund managers have not been doing very well.

Defined Contribution Plans Blossom

Because pension fund managers have had such dismal investment records, and because the needs of individual workers are so varied, defined contribution plans have picked up steam in recent years.

As we explained in Chapter 3, defined contribution plans let you decide how your retirement money will be invested. Of course, that means that you'll need to know something about each choice you face. Moreover, you'll need to have a strategy that will help you switch investment options when you sense that the economy is changing. You may worry that you'll get hurt if you stick by your original selection.

You'll be facing the same "need to know" pressure as your IRA balance starts to reach the $8,000 level. Maybe you didn't think much about investment strategy when you first plunked down the $2,000 to open your IRA. However, with your IRA balance growing, you'll need to think about diversifying your funds a bit. You might have the urge to put some of your IRA money in a higher-risk investment that promises very high capital appreciation.

The same goes for any Keogh investments you or your family members have. As account balances increase, you'll need to start paying close attention to the rate of return you're getting.

In fact, you'll need to begin to view your retirement savings—no matter where the various components are housed—as one reservoir of income that will be vital to your security.

Which Way Is Up

Is a bond fund the right choice for a portion of your retirement nest egg? What about a growth stock fund? Company stock? A money market option? Bankers talk all the time about the importance of federal deposit insurance—should you take their advice *and* their low rates of return? Stockbrokers say that zero coupon bonds are the best bet, but how do you know they're not just trying to rake in commissions?

Don't Grope in the Dark

With the investment strategy we are about to define, you can take your hard-earned retirement savings, and the contributions donated by your employer, and manage your nest egg's growth and safety with confidence.

Retirement: The Investment Opportunity of a Lifetime

Tax-sheltered retirement savings plans like IRAs, Keoghs, and 401(k) programs have some unique properties that distinguish them from other savings and investment programs:

1. If you still qualify for the IRA deduction, investing for retirement saves you money from the word "go." Your annual contribution helps reduce your current year tax bill.
2. The taxman stays completely away for decades. Because your investment earnings are tax-deferred, you can reinvest them and get supercharged compounding working for you.

Rethinking Your Strategy

What does all of this mean when you are developing an investment strategy for your retirement savings? The conclusions are fairly simple:

1. Be assertive. With supercharged compounding working for you, the timid—and the slow starters—are left in the dust.
2. Take some risk, but take it carefully. Assuming some measure of investment risk lets you shoot for relatively higher returns. Furthermore, if you lose some money, and you have sufficient time left before retirement, you can make it up more quickly in a tax-deferred investment.
3. Do your best to understand the options available to you, and select an investment that lets you build the healthiest nest egg. For example, if you no longer qualify for the IRA deduction, consider tax-deferred annuities, which do not restrict the dollar amounts you can contribute.
4. Start now with what you can afford. The sooner you can get money invested in your retirement savings plan, the better.

5. Be an early bird. If you can afford it, invest the full amount in your retirement plan on January 1 of each taxable year. Why not strive for all the tax-deferred compounding you can get?

6. Go with the best plan first. Always fully fund your 401(k) before you work on your IRA. The point is to take advantage of your employer's offer to contribute on your behalf. It won't do you much good to have a fully funded IRA if you can't afford to make contributions to your 401(k)—passing up the 401(k) may mean passing up your employer's largesse.

7. Think long-term growth, not short-term safety. If you are still young, your retirement savings plan is a long-term investment. Therefore, it doesn't make sense to put the bulk of your money in timid, short-term oriented investments, such as bank CDs. Only carefully chosen stock market investments are capable of the best long-term returns.

8. Keep your investments in tune with the times. Do not be bashful about moving your funds in or out of the stock market as economic conditions warrant. Learn how to seek maximum growth for all or a portion of your retirement money. Be prepared to switch your investments around in an effort to avoid losses. No-load mutual funds with exchange (switching) privileges will help you avoid unnecessary transaction costs.

What we've just outlined is a broad view—intended to start you thinking about investment goals and strategies for your retirement savings. Now you're ready for the specifics.

Investments 101—How the Investment Markets Work

If you listen to the news each day, you hear "The stock market is up" one day and "The stock market is down" the next. And then some economist gives some equally complex analysis of how the market could go either way tomorrow.

It's very confusing and frustrating. Many savers just give up on serious investing—you can hear them grumbling: "The stock market is for high-rollers and gamblers; I'll play it safe and put my money in the bank. Besides, this is my retirement money, and I can't afford to lose it."

It's Not That Complex

The truth is that wise investing doesn't have to be complicated— at least not over the long run. By the long run, we mean looking at your investment returns with a few years' perspective.

We know an investment adviser who thinks that the "long term" is between now and dinner. He is a true child of the money market revolution, which gave investors a taste for high, ostensibly riskless, current yields. What we all must remember is that IRA and 401(k) programs were an attempt by Congress to get people to think long-term again.

It's understandable that people without investment experience fear that if they venture beyond the bank lobby, they will lose money. If you're one of these people, what you have to keep in mind is that if you don't take some risk, you are avoiding earning money—that's a form of losing, too!

The trick is learning how to take an appropriate amount of risk and how to avoid unnecessary risks. And, remember, the risk of losing 100% of your money is minuscule (unless, of course, you're foolish enough to pour all your funds directly into the stock market based on the proverbial "hot tip").

If you take the time to understand what you're doing, and if you reach for the brass ring through mutual funds (which provide professional portfolio management and built-in diversification), your investment risk is certainly reduced—compared to the risk you take when you go into the market directly.

As a practical matter, investing through a well-respected stock market fund—one with a solid track record and one offered by a reputable firm—you're probably speculating with no more than 10% of your principal. That may sound like a lot, but you must realize that assuming some risk is the only way you can hope to achieve relatively high returns. Moreover, when you consider that the stock market is, by nature, a long-term investment, you'll see that it is, indeed, appropriate to have some portion of your retirement savings placed there.

So far, so good. We may have convinced you not to lock up all your retirement savings in low-yielding bank investments. Where do you go from here? Before we get to our nuts-and-bolts advice, you'll need to have a firm grip on recent economic events.

Recent History and Investment Secrets

During the past few years, as interest rates soared and plummeted, many investors got a short-course in investment finance. A close look at the past five years is revealing.

In the late 1970s and early 1980s, interest rates went sky-high as inflation roared out of control. (Thanks, OPEC!) It was not until interest rates declined in early 1982 that we had the fodder for a stock market rally of major proportions—that famous bull started its stampede on August 12, 1982, and kept moving for nearly a full year.

An interest rate rally (that's Wall Street-speak for rising rates) in 1983 put the kibosh on the stock market's ascent for a time. After interest rates found their peak, and returned to "normal" levels, the stock market heated up once again.

During the periods 1982–83 and 1985–86, we saw true "double your money" bull markets. By the summer of 1986, the Dow had topped the incredible 1900 mark, and the party was at a fevered pitch. However, investors received a rude awakening in mid-September, 1986, when the Dow dropped 82 points in a single day. The era of unprecedented stock market volatility had arrived, thanks to the doings of well-heeled professionals engaged in computerized program trading. Many individual investors realized they could no longer take on the risk of direct market investing—and mutual funds became all the more appealing. It's no coincidence that the Donoghue Organization unveiled its new strategy for mutual fund investing in the fall of 1986.

The Donoghue Investment Strategy

The Donoghue Investment Strategy is a multifaceted tool for selecting top-performing mutual funds and keeping your investment portfolio in tune with the markets. That means investing in stock market mutual funds when the stock market is rising, and avoiding them when stock prices are falling. No system is infallible, of course, but The Donoghue Strategy can certainly help you seize many investment opportunities—and avoid costly mistakes you'd probably incur if you flew solo.

The Donoghue Strategy can be used to manage retirement money that is invested in growth stock mutual funds. In fact, we strongly urge you to take an assertive approach to retirement investing—just because you don't plan to touch these assets until retirement does not mean you should simply sit back and hope for the best. What's more, we know that your golden years will be all the more enjoyable if you make smart investment decisions at an early age.

Some folks who are rather close to retirement may be hesitant to engage in mutual fund switching and market timing. They may be afraid to engage in what seems like an overly aggressive strategy for maximizing investment returns. Our response: We agree that you should never take on a level of investment risk that makes you uncomfortable. Nonetheless, we urge you to consider the value of strategic loss avoidance, which, as we explain below, is a cornerstone of The Donoghue Strategy. Moreover, if you decide not to apply The Donoghue Strategy to your retirement savings, you may want to consider using it to direct your nonretirement portfolio.

The Donoghue Strategy is a conservative, long-term approach in that it strives to safeguard your assets by avoiding losses. It was built on several strategic components to help you respond confidently to economic events, especially changes in interest rates. It helps you get in position for major stock market moves, both bullish and bearish. By telling you when to increase or decrease your holdings in carefully chosen equity funds—and where to invest when the stock market is on the blink—The Donoghue Strategy delivers more investment profits than you could possibly earn with the old buy-hold-pray approach.

"But is it risky?" you ask. Compared to other fonts of investment advice, The Donoghue Strategy is rather conservative in that it attempts to spot substantial, long-term market moves. We won't have you trading your portfolio of mutual funds on a daily basis. Keep in mind, however, that every approach to stock market investing involves a certain level of risk.

Finally, as we describe below how the system works, you'll see that The Donoghue Strategy is extremely easy to use. It's simple without being simplistic. You don't have to waste hour after frustrating hour attempting to decipher confusing statistics and investment legalese.

We all know now that the economy and the financial markets have changed tremendously over the past few years. And it is the nature of that change that led us to develop the next logical step for our original investment system, SLYC. We studied how the market shot to record-breaking heights and, in the process, grew so very complex and so dangerously volatile—what with program trading, portfolio insurance, risky option plays, and the like—that the job of the individual investor became darned near impossible.

We realized that investors wanted to participate in the surging bull market without losing their shirts. Folks who attended our seminars, wrote letters to our office, and subscribed to Donoghue's *MONEY-LETTER* ® all seemed to be saying loud and clear: "The current bull market is too good to be true, but direct investment in the stock market is too risky. We want to know which equity funds, low-load and no-load, will likely outperform the pack, and we want to know when it's safe to take the plunge. Moreover, we want to know when to put only a portion of our money in the stock market and when to go whole hog."

The Donoghue Strategy meets these investor needs. To see how it works, let's walk through a step-by-step, decision-making process for choosing and investing in equity mutual funds.

Fund Selection

First, you'll need a fund family that offers convenient telephone switches (and doesn't put too low a limit on the number of switches you can make before incurring a per-switch fee), a low minimum investment requirement and a low additional investment requirement, and a choice of at least a money market fund, a bond fund, and several equity funds with different approaches to the risk/return equation. If you want to switch among equity funds sold by different fund families, you may want to use the Schwab Mutual Fund Marketplace. You can open an account with the Schwab Mutual Fund Marketplace and conveniently switch among funds from different families and have instant access to the Kemper money funds. (The Kemper money funds, by the way, have been consistent top performers over the years.) As we'll see below, being able to move into a money fund with one quick phone call comes in handy when the stock market heads south. Whether you use Schwab or a fund family that offers a full menu of equity, bond, and money funds, your goal is to invest only in funds that offer instant liquidity—the ability to move your money in a day—with a simple phone call. Obviously, a toll-free 800 number is ideal. Remember, if you are transferring tax-advantaged retirement money, such as IRA assets, from one fund to another, you do not actually receive the assets and thus do not have to worry about the IRS.

How do you begin to select funds? First, refer regularly to Donoghue's Mutual Funds Almanac. Published annually, the Almanac gives crucial details on over 1,400 funds. Our twice-monthly newsletter, Donoghue's *MONEYLETTER*®, reports on the performance of 35 funds included in our carefully selected "fund universe" and lists the ones we think are especially hot. *MONEYLETTER*® has recently been redesigned to include Donoghue's Recommendations—a list of our current buy, hold, and sell signals. Although we now include low-load funds with stellar returns, we suggest that you go the no-load route when their returns are competitive. After all, why pay a 3 percent sales charge when a no-load fund is just as good? (We'll bet that our newsletter currently has a "sell" recommendation on a fund you now own.) Donoghue's *MONEYLETTER*® also notes funds we currently do not recommend. (For a free sample, call 1-800-343-5413.)

Our specific advice on which equity funds promise to beat the pack —and which funds are preparing for a nosedive—is based on our analysis of fund performance over three key time periods: four weeks, six months, and twelve months. (We considered longer time periods, such as five years, but tests showed they did not provide useful data on which funds will outperform the competition in the near future.) To this analysis we apply a weighting factor, which identifies the consistent winners and at the same time weeds out "flash in the pan" funds that occasionally land by fluke on our four-week, top ten list. We assign each fund a numerical rank, which reflects overall fund performance by taking into account the different time periods. The ranking lets you choose funds that have delivered consistent top performance.

When we developed The Donoghue Strategy, we knew that a ranking system based purely on past performance only gets you halfway there. So, we designed a built-in trend confirmation system that attempts to spot funds that will likely provide consistent, strong returns in the future and, just as important, spot funds that are losing position and will likely remain back in the pack.

Like any other system forecasting future relative performance, the Donoghue approach stubs its toe now and then, but it does so infrequently. If a fund is a consistently good performer, our tracking system will pick it up, and we will continue to recommend it as long as it delivers a relatively attractive investment result. On the other hand, if one of our buys ceases to perform and stumbles badly, our tracking system will quickly flag it, and we will recommend that you move out of that fund. The beauty of the system is that it is dynamic —it moves you in and out of funds according to how they are performing. Our system helps you avoid painful losses and those sleepless nights that come from investing in a fund just before it slumps and then waiting—perhaps forever—for it to rebound, so you can at least break even.

It's important to note that The Donoghue Strategy is not built on a hair trigger. From our extensive testing, we know that the system does not change its buy-and-sell list with every twist of the stock market. The Donoghue Strategy is by nature geared for long-term investment profits.

Moving in Time

The mention of market twists and turns brings us to the final component of The Donoghue Strategy, our system for timing major stock market moves. A lot has been written lately about this business of timing the market. Magazine articles attempt to describe this or that timing system—they come in a variety of shapes and sizes. Often, readers are left confused about what "timing the market" really means. Let's set the record straight. The purpose of market timing is to take advantage of two important investment techniques: avoiding losses and improving the efficiency of compounding investment returns. When we say timing, we refer to an investment strategy that tries to allocate money, either totally or partially, in the stock market at the most lucrative times. Obviously, you want to load up on promising stock funds just when the bull is about to take off. (Remember, a bull market can last months or years.) At such a time, share prices are relatively low, and you stand to earn serious profits. One trick, however, is selling out near the top and preserving your capital. If you can do that, you avoid the big decline and, more importantly, are prepared to buy back in at bargain prices after the market has dropped. That way, your money compounds its investment returns at higher and higher rates.

When the bull is tuckered out, you want to seek shelter in the money market, where the value of your principal does not fluctuate and your money earns current money market rates. At such a time, the idea is to avoid painful stock market declines and get your money earning a decent return in the money market—not the negative returns produced by a retreating bull. This is the essence of market timing: adding incremental return to what would otherwise be gained through the old buy-hold-pray approach.

Finally, when the market is, as they say on Wall Street, trading sideways (going neither up nor down but fluttering a lot), you may want to have some portion of your money in the stock market and some in the money market. When the American stock market is looking shaky and/or trading sideways, and there are indications that economies overseas may offer strong investment rewards, you may also want to have some of your money invested in an international growth stock fund. Such a fund invests in promising companies in other countries. (Worried about being an unpatriotic investor? Isn't that a Honda in your driveway?)

How can we tell when the time is right to move money in or out of the U.S. stock market? That's the key question for all market timing systems. You should realize that no system, including ours, can call every market top and bottom perfectly. A good system, however, based as it should be on sound economic principles and managed by market experts, can help get you in the stock market when strong gains are possible, and get you out when the weather turns nasty. We have done extensive testing of our past market performance, and because of this, we know that The Donoghue Strategy should do the trick. It has shown that it can beat the performance of the S&P 500, a traditional benchmark, and we are confident that its underlying indicators, when analyzed by our team of experts, can identify long-term market trends.

While we believe The Donoghue Strategy will help you become a successful and confident investor, we want you to keep in mind that, like all systems, it has been tested against past market results. There's no way to guarantee that the market will always perform as it has in the past. Any system that tries to entice you with such guarantees is a fraud.

The Technicals of Timing

Here's how our system works. Our calls are based on an analysis of three long-term indicators of major stock market moves. By major, we mean moves that represent at least a 10% fluctuation in the Dow

Jones Industrial Average. A 10% change in the Dow, by the way, would include so-called market corrections. (Other timing systems, which try to catch every small turn of the market, are really only appropriate for the "pros" who work for institutional investors such as pension funds and brokerage houses.)

Every indicator has its own strengths and weaknesses. Some are good at predicting market tops (sell signals), others are good at market bottoms (buy signals). We chose a mix of indicators that would enable us to call both market tops and bottoms. Our indicators have also shown, through extensive testing, an ability to give clear signals. In other words, when we signal that the bull is ready to go on a rampage (or, conversely, slump down in the grass), we're real sure about it. When a market surge is about to occur, we tell you to invest 100 percent in equities. When the most recent bull market is on its last legs, we tell you to move 100 percent into the money market until a new bull appears on the field. Finally, when our indicators disagree, we know that we're probably in for a spell of sideways trading. At such a time, we recommend that you allocate various portions of your money between the stock and money markets. As well, international stock funds may be recommended. The ultimate goal at such a time is to have some participation in the stock market, but maintain a healthy margin of safety by sheltering some of your dollars in the money market.

Readers of all three previous Donoghue books, and our latest best-seller, *William E. Donoghue's Lifetime Financial Planner,* will recognize the phrase "money fund average maturity." Our original SLYC system recommended investment positions based on where interest rates were headed. It was, and remains, our view that the direction of interest rates drives the stock market. When we used SLYC to time the market, we knew where interest rates were heading by watching for changes in the average maturity of money funds.

The Donoghue Strategy described here builds on that tradition— one of its indicators is the average maturity figure for institutions-only money funds. (These special money funds are only available to large institutional investors.) We chose that indicator over the average maturity figure for all money funds because we have found—again through extensive testing—that it is much more sensitive to interest rate trends and, therefore, a better predictor of imminent stock market moves. You can see that The Donoghue Strategy, which was unveiled in late 1986, has its roots in our earlier work.

How can you put The Donoghue Strategy to work for you? First, decide how much you can afford as an initial investment, then get your hands on a current copy of Donoghue's *MONEYLETTER*®. On page 1 you will find a list of the stock mutual funds that we feel offer the strongest potential returns. Check page 3 for the box entitled "Current Advice." This tells three types of investors (conservative, active, and venturesome) exactly what percentage of money should be placed in U.S. stock funds, what percentage in international stock funds, and what percentage in a money fund. Our economic commentary offers a detailed rationale for our current positions. By the way, when you subscribe, you fill out a "risk questionnaire," which helps you decide whether you're a conservative, active, or venturesome investor.

Our original SLYC system was very much do-it-yourself. In past books, we taught you how to gauge interest rate trends by watching for changes in a very special number: the average maturity of money market mutual funds. The Donoghue Organization compiles that statistic weekly, and it is published in newspapers nationwide. As we mentioned earlier, the financial markets have become extremely complex and volatile—today, you need more than the average maturity number. Quite frankly, the only way you can keep on top of things is to receive regular, expert advice on market trends and fund performance.

What's the value of expert advice? If you had invested in the top five growth stock funds tracked by Donoghue's *MONEYLETTER*®, and if you switched among stock and money funds according to our recommendations, you could have earned, on average, over 26% annually from June 1981 to June 1986.

9 Selecting Your Pension Payout Plan

Well, congratulations. You've put in your time, earned your gold stars and your gold watch. Now you can study Japanese, take up oil painting, travel to Aruba, or simply spend time with your grandchildren. The time has come to enjoy the retirement life-style you've dreamed about for so long. With a little luck—and sound career and financial planning behind you—you should now have a substantial pension account to your credit. As well, you should have a healthy IRA account, maybe even a Keogh and some valuable investments to draw on.

In this chapter, we'll explain the legal rules about receiving your pension from your employer's pension plan. (For information about Keogh plans for the self-employed, see Chapter 6; for IRA facts, see Chapter 2.)

Lump Sum vs. Annuity

If your employer's plan is like most plans, you have two choices for receiving the amount in your pension account: as a lump sum, or as an annuity (regular monthly payments). As a result of a 1984 statute called the Retirement Equity Act, if your employer offers annuities at all, you must have a choice between receiving a "single life annuity" (which stops at the death of the employee) or a "joint and survivor annuity" (which makes payments for the lives of both the employee and his or her spouse—in this case, because payments are likely to go on longer, each monthly payment will be smaller). Moreover, you'll need the consent of your spouse to give up the joint and survivor annuity option.

In addition to annuities measured by lifetimes, you can also choose an annuity payable for a certain number of years—even if you die in the interim, payments will continue to the beneficiary you designated. You can pick the number of years—as long as you don't pick a number of years longer than the joint life expectancies of you and your spouse. Once again, the trade-off will be that the longer the period of time over which payments are made, the smaller each payment will be.

Most people will choose either to receive a lump-sum payout or to have the employer provide an annuity. However, there is another choice for retirees who have not yet reached 70½: They can defer taxation even longer by rolling over the amount of the pension payout into an IRA (see Chapter 2). Of course, they will have to pay taxes as soon as they start taking money out of the IRA, or as soon as they reach 70½, retired or not. The point is that you can't put off paying the piper forever.

We just want to mention that possibility, in case you have plenty of other income and want to defer taxes to the last permissible moment. If you fit this profile, discuss the IRA rollover option with your accountant. You'll want to be certain that your overall tax planning strategy is not disrupted.

What's Best for You?

Almost everyone needs monthly income from his retirement funds to meet immediate expenses as soon as he retires. So, we'll discuss the financial and tax ramifications of either taking a lump-sum distribution or leaving the pension funds with the employer's pension plan and receiving an annuity.

Although the choice is a very individual one, there are some guidelines that frequently apply. You might want to choose a lump-sum payout if:

- You have a history of success as an investor, and you think you can do better by investing the lump sum than you can by relying on the investment skills of the corporate pension trustees. Remember, they have to be extremely conservative in their investments; therefore they can never get really high returns.
- You need the cash for medical bills, college costs, to pay off your mortgage, buy a new home, or even to start a business.
- Taking the lump sum and using five-year forward averaging may give you optimal tax results. (If you were fifty years old on January 1, 1986, you can qualify to use ten-year forward averaging, but, remember, you'll be paying the higher tax rates stipulated by the old tax code. See Chapter 3.)

Of course, you can take the lump sum and buy an annuity from an insurance company—or invest the lump sum in a mutual fund that sends you a check every month—if you want a steady stream of monthly income.

On the other hand, you might consider sticking with the company pension plan and receiving the regular annuity payment it provides —if:

- You're gun-shy about investing and don't want to bother with tracking your investment's performance, economic events, and the direction of interest rates. You'd rather just stick your head in the sand and hope for the best.
- You've been an active investor all your life—you've learned all you can about money management services and why certain ones outperform others at different times (maybe you subscribe to Donoghue's *MONEYLETTER*®!) but you just want the peace of mind that annuity payments provide.
- You're not at all intimidated by investing in mutual funds, but you're simply pessimistic about economic trends. And, so, you think the guaranteed monthly income from the pension annuity provided by a defined benefit plan is a better return than you'd get from individual investments, even wisely chosen ones.
- You like the security of knowing income will continue throughout

your lifetime, or the lifetime of you and your spouse. Or, you like knowing that income will continue for a certain number of years, even if you're no longer alive.

You have to make a decision that feels right to you, all things considered. But we feel the need to remind you that there is always something of a gamble involved in any decision of this kind. On the one hand, taking your pension in a lump sum and investing it— whether in a bank, mutual funds, or government bonds—calls for a sound approach to investment risk and proactive wealth preservation (see Chapters 7 and 8). On the other hand, by taking your pension in the form of an annuity, you essentially delegate to someone else the responsibility for managing a vital part of your retirement nest egg. While annuities are generally considered very safe, the fact remains that an annuity is only as safe as the company issuing it.

Okay, the Annuity Route: Now What

Most people will choose the joint and survivor annuity rather than the single-life annuity. However, the single-life annuity could be a better choice if

- your spouse will have adequate income from his or her own salary and retirement benefits, Social Security, your estate, and life insurance (remember, single-life annuity benefits stop with your death).
- you need higher income in the early years of your retirement, perhaps to make those last few mortgage payments or to clean up the last of the college bills for your kids (or their kids).

But if the pension and Social Security will be the only substantial income you and your spouse have during retirement, the joint and survivor annuity is almost certainly the better choice. Otherwise, your spouse could be left with very little income or resources after your death.

10 The Seniors' Guide to Medical Care Payments

"If I knew I was going to live this long," the old joke goes, "I would have taken better care of myself." If you're reading this when you're in your twenties or thirties, maybe you'll take this to heart and stop smoking, cut back on drinking and eating unhealthy foods, and adopt a sensible exercise program. Even if you're in your forties, fifties, or sixties, you can do a lot to improve your health and mobility.

But, let's face it, you are only human. (Your authors are only human.) And even the best-maintained human organism is going to need some medical "fine tuning" sooner or later. Maybe you'll go out in a blaze of glory, piloting your own plane when you're 103. But, while that's possible, it's not probable. As you get older, the chances are excellent that you'll suffer from at least one chronic ailment. You may need to be hospitalized one or more times, and you may need to enter a nursing home—perhaps because you're recuperating from an operation, or because you're too physically weak or mentally confused to live independently.

Sometimes, the Best-laid Plans

We're sure you realize how personally devastating such illnesses can be to the person who suffers them, and to his or her spouse, children, family, and friends. But what you probably *don't* realize is that chronic illness is almost certain to be financially devastating, often wiping out the savings of a lifetime. Many people have established savings programs, made intelligent investment choices, made tax-wise estate plans—and have seen them all evaporated by medical costs.

Young readers can take steps to protect themselves by acting *now*. This may not seem very crucial, or have a very high priority. But older readers, or younger readers concerned about their parents' medical and financial needs, will find it a lot easier psychologically to take the necessary steps.

Disaster Recovery Planning

A lot can be done to protect a family's assets against medical costs —provided that plans are made far enough in advance. Steps, though less effective, can be taken once a person is aged and ill. The longer you wait to plan, the less that can be done to protect you. The key is to find a good lawyer who thoroughly understands trust law and the way the Medicaid and Medicare laws and rules are administered in your state. (It can take a long time just to find a lawyer with the necessary expertise.) This is not a do-it-yourself process; what you need is a very sophisticated lawyer who also has some degree of financial savvy.

"Doesn't Medicare Pay for That?"

In theory, when the Medicare program was created two decades ago, it was supposed to cope with all medical care problems of senior citizens. But the way the law was written reflects a subtle but pervasive ageism (bias against the elderly). Medicare is keyed to treatment of acute illnesses—isolated episodes like heart attacks and injuries caused by automobile accidents. But most older people have one or more chronic illnesses—such as high blood pressure that needs regular monitoring, gradually deteriorating vision or hearing, arthritis, or other disease. Some older people (though by no means all) need assistance with daily tasks like shopping, cooking, bathing, or getting dressed, or they need to live in a facility that provides custodial as well as medical care.

Medicare is, in essence, a health insurance program, but most people don't think of it that way because only one part of Medicare carries a noticeable "insurance premium."

Medicare Part A pays for hospitalization and convalescence after a hospital stay (either in a skilled nursing home or at home, with home nursing and health aides).

In general, anyone over 65 (not necessarily retired) who collects or is eligible for Social Security benefits is entitled to Part A, and there's no specific charge for it. Those who collect Social Security benefits are automatically enrolled in Part A; those who are eligible but don't yet collect must apply for Part A. Workers who are over 65 but under 69 can agree to substitute Medicare for their employer's health insurance plan as the primary payer for hospital costs.

Part A will pay for up to 90 days of hospitalization during a "spell of illness" (and for any number of "spells of illness"). Each Part A patient also gets a total of 60 extra days of hospitalization coverage that can be applied to spells of illness that last more than 90 days. Problems can arise if a person gets sick, is hospitalized, leaves the hospital, goes to a nursing home, and then gets sick again. Medicare officials may claim that a new "spell of illness" has not started so Part A coverage is unavailable for the second hospitalization. In this case, the patient (or his or her family) should get in touch with a lawyer skilled in Medicare litigation—excellent results have been obtained by litigation, or even by threatening litigation.

Part A pays for nursing care in the hospital (but not for private-duty nurses), and for drugs furnished to the patient while he or she is in the hospital.

Therein Lies the Rub

Medicare Part B seems more like conventional health insurance because a separate premium is charged for it. As of January, 1987, the premium was $17.90 per month. It's deducted automatically from Social Security checks unless the Social Security beneficiary refuses to participate in Part B. The premiums are paid by the government for older people receiving Medicaid or SSI (programs for the indigent). People who are not yet receiving Social Security but want to participate in Medicare can arrange to pay the premiums themselves. For full coverage, they should enroll at the local Social Security office within the three months *before* their sixty-fifth birthdays.

Medicare Part B pays for doctor bills, outpatient services in hospitals (e.g., emergency room care), medical tests, ambulance service, and drugs administered by doctors—not ordinary prescription drugs.

Deductibles and Coinsurance

Even if Medicare pays for a particular kind of medical or hospital care, it probably won't pay for all of it. For example, when a person is hospitalized, he or she must pay a "deductible" of $400 for each spell of illness. That is, the patient must pay $400 before Medicare pays anything.

If the spell of illness lasts more than 60 days, the patient must pay $100 a day "coinsurance," and if the patient uses any of the 60 lifetime reserve days, the coinsurance amount is $200 a day.

Under Part B, participants must pay a $75 a year deductible before Medicare will pay at all, and they must pay at least 20% of each doctor bill. That's because Medicare pays 80% of what it considers to be the reasonable charge for a particular service—the doctor may have an entirely different idea about what's a reasonable charge, and he or she may bill a lot more, leaving the patient responsible for the difference.

Cost-cutting Measures

Medicare took dramatic (not necessarily well-advised) steps to cut medical costs in 1985. It adopted a Diagnosis Related Groups (DRG) system for paying hospitals for caring for Medicare patients, and instituted a fee freeze for Part B.

Before DRG, hospitals got paid for Medicare patients on the basis of a complex calculation involving the hospital's cost of providing care. As you can imagine, this encouraged them to provide care as expensively as possible (though the extra cost didn't necessarily do anything for the patients). The DRG system divides all human ailments into 470 diagnoses. The hospital gets paid a basic amount, according to the patient's diagnosis, not on how long he or she spends in the hospital or what treatment he or she receives.

Medicare Madness

Now hospitals have an incentive to treat patients as *cheaply* as possible, and charges have been made that the patients are being discharged before they're well enough to go home and without available nursing home facilities to take care of them in the interim. The system also opens up new vistas for outright fraud, since a hospital can make more money by claiming that a particular patient falls into a highly paid DRG than into a more modest one.

About one-quarter of all physicians are "participating physicians" under Medicare. That is, they agree to bill Medicare directly (instead of billing the patient, making the patient get the money back from Medicare, which can be a lengthy and difficult process) and to accept the Medicare "reasonable charge" as their full charge.

Medicare imposed a fee freeze for doctors between July 1, 1984, and September 31, 1985. Nonparticipating doctors were not allowed to charge their Medicare patients more than they charged them in the period April 1–June 30, 1984. (Whatever they charged then or charge now, Medicare still pays only 80% of its reasonable charge.)

Furthermore, after the freeze, nonparticipating doctors were not allowed to raise fees even if they were based on 1985 cost increases, but the "reasonable charges" accepted by participating physicians will be adjusted for 1985 costs. If your doctor is nonparticipating, and he or she raised fees for Medicare patients during the freeze, complain to the federal Department of Health and Human Services (which includes Medicare). The culprit may have to pay fines, or even be barred from getting money from Medicare for five years.

What Medicare Doesn't Cover

Medicare covers hospitalization and convalescence after a hospital stay. It provides limited benefits for home health care—again, related to an acute illness. Much of the home care older people need (help with housekeeping, for instance) is not covered.

Neither Part A nor Part B will cover:

- checkups.
- eye exams, eyeglasses, or contact lenses.
- hearing exams or hearing aids.
- orthopedic shoes or foot care.
- dental care or dentures.
- prescription drugs that are *not* administered by a doctor. In other words, if your doctor gives you an injection, that's covered, but a prescription for pills is not covered. However, some states have programs that pay part of the cost of prescriptions for older people.
- nursing home care that is custodial—not related to recuperation from a hospital stay.

Notice that many of these things are necessary for older people to be able to live independently and to be reasonably mobile. Also notice that the average senior citizen will spend a great deal of money each year on health care that is not covered by Medicare. If he or she does need care that is Medicare-eligible, he or she will still have to pay the deductibles and coinsurance. Meeting the cost of ordinary health care will be difficult for senior citizens, unless they're quite well-to-do. Meeting the cost of a serious illness will be financially crippling even if the medical outcome is excellent. Are there *any* alternatives to either doing without necessary care or becoming impoverished?

Medi-Gap Insurance

About two-thirds of Medicare beneficiaries have "Medi-Gap" insurance designed to supplement Medicare by paying the deductibles and coinsurance, and by paying for services that are not covered by Medicare. However, it's almost impossible to buy insurance that will pay for long-term custodial care.

Some Medi-Gap policies are individual policies, some are group policies. The group policies tend to be more comprehensive, but are also more expensive than individual policies.

First, you'll want to distinguish between ethical insurance companies offering valid policies, and fly-by-nights out to defraud old people. State insurance commissioners regulate Medi-Gap policies, and some states (such as New York) rate Medi-Gap policies.

The National Association of Insurance Commissioners (NAIC) has adopted model standards for these policies. The Health Care Finance Administration (the part of the Department of Health and Human Services that actually runs the Medicare program) has a program for certifying Medi-Gap policies. If a policy conforms to the NAIC's standards, and if most of the premiums are used to provide benefits for the insured (not to run the company or swell its profits), the policy can carry a seal of approval. If someone tries to sell you a Medi-Gap policy that *doesn't* have the seal of approval, find out why it doesn't.

Of course, Medi-Gap isn't the only form of insurance that can be helpful to senior citizens. Many employers will continue to cover retired workers under their health-care insurance plan. People who buy major medical insurance coverage may be able to maintain the coverage throughout their lives at rates comparable to rates for Medi-Gap policies. These forms of insurance coverage are especially important if one spouse is eligible for Medicare but the other isn't—is too young, for example, and doesn't have adequate health insurance coverage from his or her job. In that situation, neither Medicare nor Medi-Gap policies will take care of the younger spouse's medical needs.

Medicaid

Many older people find that they've used up their Medicare coverage, that they need care not covered by Medicare (and for which they lack private insurance), or they've used up their private insurance. Even if they're willing to pay out of their own pockets, the cost is likely to be crushing. Serious surgery costs as much as a Cadillac; nursing home bills *start* at about $20,000 a year, and can easily exceed $60,000 a year.

There *is* a government program that pays many of these catastrophic bills, but it's a very unattractive one. The Medicaid program pays medical bills, with no deductible or coinsurance—but Medicaid is a program for the indigent.

People who are receiving Welfare, Social Security disability, or Supplemental Security Income are eligible for Medicaid. Depending on the state, people who are "medically indigent" (can't afford to pay their medical bills) may be eligible for Medicaid as well. The rules are very complicated, and consultation with an expert lawyer is most helpful. Of course, indigent people can't afford private lawyers, and public-service lawyers are few, far between, and burdened by heavy caseloads.

In order to qualify as indigent, a person who applies for Medicaid must have an income below a certain level (again, it varies from state to state) and must have resources below a certain level. However, some resources are *exempt* (not counted in determining the level of assets). The most important exempt resource is a person's home. If he or she owns a home and lives in it (i.e., it is not an investment property), the home's value is not included in determining resources. Neither is the value of wedding or engagement rings.

Where there's a rule, there's a loophole, and lawyers can do a lot to transfer property so that it will not be counted in determining eligibility for Medicaid. But the process is a subtle one, fraught with difficulty. For one thing, any transfer made within two years of the time a person applies for Medicaid is presumed to be made *just* in order to qualify for Medicaid; the state Medicaid agency may have a legal right to disregard the transfer, and deny Medicaid to the person who made the transfer. There are also pitfalls of "spousal responsibility" and "deeming" to overcome.

Deeming and Spousal Responsibility

Let's assume that an older person is very ill or needs nursing home placement. He or she, or his or her family, are likely to apply for Medicaid to pay the bills. The local Medicaid agency will apply its own rules to determine if the sick person is eligible for Medicaid. The sick person may have to prove that he or she has no substantial nonexempt assets. Sometimes, it may be enough to prove that he or she has extraordinarily high medical bills.

The Medicaid agency will also look at transfers of property made in the two years before the application, to see if they can be disregarded. You'd think that the simplest thing would be for the sick person to transfer all of his or her assets to the spouse. That way, the spouse has money to live on, the sick person qualifies for Medicaid, and everybody's happy (except Medicaid).

Unfortunately, Medicaid agencies will *deem* (consider) each spouse's resources eligible to the other spouse for a period of time after the Medicaid application. This is likely to mean that Medicaid payments will be unavailable for several months. To pay the bills for these months, the couple will have to use funds they planned to leave to their children, funds needed for a comfortable retirement, and even funds needed for day-to-day decent living.

But the nightmare isn't over yet. Let's say that the sick spouse finally qualifies for Medicaid. The local Medicaid agency may sue the "community" spouse (the healthy spouse living in the community, not in a nursing home) for nonsupport, trying to force him or her to reimburse Medicaid for the money it spends. That's because both spouses have a legal obligation to support one another—it's not just a husband's obligation to support his wife. Looking on the bright side, a lot of Medicaid agencies are too overworked and understaffed to bring nonsupport actions.

Even if he or she isn't sued for nonsupport, the community spouse can have terrible problems: Once all the family's assets have been spent on medical care, how can he or she pay the mortgage, buy food, take care of his or her own medical needs? Without planning, there's very little he or she can do. With planning, many of these problems can be avoided, or at least have their impact softened.

Planning Ahead

One of the problems of old age is that some of the ailments and infirmities that attack people are physical, some are mental. In order to have the legal capacity to make a contract or draw up a trust, a person must be mentally alert and understand his or her business transactions and their legal and practical consequences. A person suffering from Alzheimer's disease, or from hardening of the arteries of the brain, may not be able to do this. To get around this problem, people can set up trusts and other legal arrangements while they're still young and have the necessary mental capacity; they can also use *powers of attorney*.

Powers of Attorney

A power of attorney is a legal document that authorizes one person to act for another. For example, a person's spouse or business partner can be delegated to take care of the person's business affairs while he or she is on a trip. The basic rule of law is that a power of attorney loses its legal effect if the person who signed it becomes legally incompetent. To get around this, all the states now allow what is called a *durable power of attorney*—one which stays effective even after the signer becomes incompetent. But the power of attorney must say, explicitly, that it's durable.

Some states even allow a *springing power of attorney:* one which doesn't become effective *until* a person becomes incompetent. So a person can retain control over his or her property and investments *until* he or she becomes incompetent, when someone else takes over.

With a power of attorney in place, the person designated as the agent can set up a trust, make gifts, pay bills, and otherwise manage the financial affairs of an incapacitated person. The power of attorney is effective automatically, and there's no need for a time-consuming, expensive procedure to appoint a guardian. Furthermore, the in-capacitated person's affairs are managed by someone he or she chose, following his or her instructions—not someone appointed by a court.

Trusts

Medicaid looks to a person's available assets (and, to a certain extent, to those of his or her spouse). Some assets, like the family home, are exempt. Other assets are not considered available.

Lawyers evolved trust strategies to get around the iron grip of the Medicaid rules. One popular technique was to have a person who might later need Medicaid transfer substantial assets to an irrevocable trust (one that can't be canceled). (Assets in a revocable trust are always considered available for Medicaid purposes, because the person who set up the trust can get the assets back by revoking the trust.) The technique called for the transferor to have no right to demand money from the trust; instead, he or she would take whatever money the trustee decided to give him. The whole trick was to choose a friendly trustee who would always decide to give the transferor plenty of money.

However, a 1985 law called COBRA (the Comprehensive Omni-bus Budget Reconciliation Act) made this a lot harder to do, by changing Medicaid law to treat *any* amount a trustee could choose to give out as an available asset—not just amounts actually paid out. This makes planning a lot harder—but don't give up. If you give a bunch of lawyers long enough, they'll find a way to prove that a three-pound pumpkin is an Audi 5000.

If children give money to their parents, the money is considered an available asset. On the other hand, if the children buy a house, co-op or condo and let the parents live in it, neither the cost of the house nor the mortgage payments are available assets for the parents. The kids get a tax deduction for the interest they pay, and—provided that they charge their parents a fair-market rent—the kids become, in effect, landlords, and are therefore entitled to the same tax advantages any landlord gets.

If you're young and healthy and concerned about your own future, or about the future of your parents, by all means consult a lawyer about durable powers of attorney, irrevocable trusts, and tax-wise strategies for helping your parents with their expenses. If you're nearing retirement age or retired, get legal advice right away. Today's actions may make all the difference between comfortable retirement and poverty for you and your spouse.

Housing Strategies and Medicaid

People over 55 who sell their principal residences can get up to $125,000 of tax-free profit. That's very tempting, especially if the big ol' house is too hard to clean, heat, and maintain. But think twice before selling your home unless you buy another home. Remember, a home is an exempt asset, so your spouse will have a place to live if you need nursing home placement. The fact that you own a home (even an expensive one) won't be used to deny Medicaid benefits.

A widow or widower may be inclined to sell the home, because there's no longer a need to furnish a home for a spouse. However, continued home ownership provides at least some assets that can be left to your children, even if all your other assets are depleted.

A few banks offer what is known as an RAM, or Reverse Annuity Mortgage. The bank pays *you* a monthly annuity; when you and your spouse die, the bank "inherits" the house in repayment of the money it advanced. You get a stable monthly income—one which *doesn't* affect your Medicaid eligibility, because Medicaid considers the whole arrangement a debt rather than income to the recipient.

Strategies for the Community Spouse

It's bad enough when a beloved spouse becomes seriously ill and has to enter a nursing home. No need to make it worse by impoverishing the spouse who remains in the community. But unless you take active steps to prevent it, this very common scenario is likely to occur. What can you do to protect yourself and your spouse?

- Get a divorce. Not only is this personally undesirable, it still leaves the sick spouse Medicaid-ineligible for the last few months of the marriage (based on deeming). Not exactly a first choice.
- In some states (New York is one) the community spouse can simply refuse to pay the sick spouse's nursing home bills. The state will stop deeming as soon as he or she does this. The Medicaid agency can still sue for nonsupport—but you can cross that bridge when you get to it.
- Turnabout is fair play—the community spouse can sue the *sick* spouse for nonsupport. The court hearing the nonsupport case is likely to make some of the couple's income and assets available for the community spouse.

With any luck at all, you'll enjoy a healthy, vigorous retirement. But if your luck runs out, there's no reason why all your money should too. The legal system offers ways to shelter your assets from medical care costs. Use them—while you're writing to your legislators to suggest changes in the expensive and tyrannical Medicaid system.

A Final Word

The Donoghue Organization, Inc., is not a law firm, nor is it a counseling service for individuals. Although we asked several experts in the field to review this chapter, it should not be viewed as a legal brief or opinion. It was our intention to provide you with an overview of the issues to guide you and your lawyer in dealing with these uncomfortable and difficult problems. We regret that we are unable to answer questions on these legal issues or provide referrals through our office.

Appendix A

Firm	SLYC Funds	Money Market Mutual Funds
AMA Advisers, Inc. 5 Sentry Parkway West Suite 120 P.O. Box 1111 Blue Bell, PA 19422 (800) 523-0864 (215) 825-0400 (PA-collect)	AMA Advisers: Medical Technology Fund	AMA M.F./Prime Port. AMA M.F./Treas. Port.
Jones & Babson Inc. 2440 Pershing Road G-15 Kansas City, MO 64108 (800) 821-5591 (816) 471-5200	Babson Growth Fund	Babson M.M.F. Federal Port. Babson M.M.F. Prime Port. Babson Tax-Free Income Fund M.M.P.
Boston Company Fund Dist., Inc. 31 St. James Avenue Boston, MA 02116 (800) 225-5267 (617) 956-9740	Boston Co. Capital Appreciation Fund	Boston Co. Cash Mgt. Boston Co. Gov't M.F. Boston Co. MA Tax-Free Fund Boston Co. Tax-Free M.F.
Bull & Bear Group, Inc. 11 Hanover Square New York, NY 10005 (800) 847-4200 (212) 363-1100	Bull & Bear Capital Growth Fund	Bull & Bear Dollar Reserves
Columbia Management Co. P.O. Box 1350 Portland, OR 97207 (800) 547-1037 (503) 222-3600 (OR-collect)	Columbia Growth Fund	Columbia Daily Income

Firm	SLYC Funds	Money Market Mutual Funds
Dreyfus Service Corp. II 666 Old Country Road Garden City, NY 11530 (800) 645-6561 (516) 794-5200 (718) 895-1206 (NYC)	Dreyfus Growth Opportunity Fund Dreyfus Third Century Fund	Dreyfus Liquid Assets Dreyfus M.M. Instruments Gov't Dreyfus Tax-Exempt M.M.F.
Fidelity Investments Corp. 82 Devonshire Street Boston, MA 02109 (800) 544-6666 (617) 523-1919 (MA-collect)	Fidelity Contrafund Fidelity Discoverer Fund	Fidelity Cash Reserves Fidelity Daily Income Fidelity U.S. Gov't Reserves Fidelity Mass. T-F/M.M.P. Fidelity Tax-Exempt M.M. Trust
Financial Programs, Inc. P.O. Box 2040 Denver, CO 80201 (800) 332-9145 (CO) (800) 525-9831 (303) 779-1233	Financial Dynamics Fund	Financial Daily Income Shares Financial Tax-Free M.F.
Founders Mutual Depositor Corp. 3033 E. First Avenue Suite 810 Denver, CO 80206 (800) 525-2440 (800) 874-6301 (CO)	Founders Growth Fund Founders Special Fund	Founders Money Market
Janus Capital Corp., Inc. 100 Fillmore Street Suite 300 Denver, CO 80206 (800) 525-3713 (303) 333-3863	Janus Fund	Cash Equivalent Fund

Firm	SLYC Funds	Money Market Mutual Funds
Lexington Management Corp. P.O. Box 1515 Saddle Brook, NJ 07662 (800) 526-0057 (201) 845-7300	Lexington Growth Fund Lexington Research Fund	Lexington Gov't Securities M.M.F. Lexington Money Market Lexington Tax-Free M.F., Inc.
SAFECO Asset Management Co. P.O. Box 34890 Seattle, WA 98124 (800) 426-6730 (800) 562-6810 (WA) (206) 545-5530	SAFECO Growth Fund	SAFECO M.M.M.F. SAFECO Tax-Free M.M.F.
Scudder Stevens & Clark 175 Federal Street Boston, MA 02110 (800) 453-3305 (617) 482-3990 (MA-collect)	Scudder Capital Growth Fund Scudder Development Fund Scudder International Fund	Scudder Cash Investment Trust Scudder Government M.F. Scudder Tax-Free M.F.
Stein Roe & Farnham P.O. Box 1143 Chicago, IL 60690 (800) 621-0320 (312) 368-7826 (IL-collect)	Stein Roe & Farnham Capital Opportunities Fund Stein Roe Special Fund Stein Roe & Farnham Stock Fund Stein Roe Universe Fund	SteinRoe Cash Reserves SteinRoe Gov't Reserves SteinRoe Tax-Exempt M.F.
T. Rowe Price Associates, Inc. 100 E. Pratt Street Baltimore, MD 21202 (800) 638-5660 (301) 547-2308 (MD-collect)	T. Rowe Price Growth Stock Fund T. Rowe Price International Fund T. Rowe Price New Era Fund T. Rowe Price New Horizons Fund	T. Rowe Price Prime Reserve T. Rowe Price U.S. Treas. M.F. T. Rowe Price T-E M.F.

Firm	SLYC Funds	Money Market Mutual Funds
USAA Investment Management Co. 9800 Fredricksburg Road San Antonio, TX 78288 (800) 531-8181 (800) 292-8181 (TX) (512) 498-7270	USAA Mutual Growth Fund USAA Sunbelt Era Fund	USAA Federal Securities M.M.F. USAA Money Market Fund USAA Tax-Exempt M.M.F.
Value Line Securities, Inc. 711 Third Avenue New York, NY 10017 (800) 223-0818 (212) 687-3965	Value Line Fund Value Line Leveraged Growth Investors Value Line Special Situations	Value Line Cash Fund Value Line Tax-Exempt Fund
Vanguard Group P.O. Box 2600 Valley Forge, PA 19496 (800) 662-7447 (215) 648-6000	Vanguard Explorer Fund Vanguard Morgan Growth Fund Vanguard Windsor Fund	Vanguard M.M.T. Federal Vanguard M.M.T. Insured Port. Vanguard M.M.T. Prime Vanguard Muni. Bond M.M.

Appendix B
Compounded Savings Interest Rate Table

| Nominal Annual Rate | The True Annual Rate If Compounded. . . . | | | | |
	Semi-Annually	Quarterly	Monthly	Weekly	Daily
3.00	3.0225	3.0339	3.0415	3.0445	3.0453
3.25	3.2764	3.2898	3.2988	3.3023	3.3032
3.50	3.5306	3.5462	3.5566	3.5607	3.5617
3.75	3.7851	3.8030	3.8151	3.8197	3.8209
4.00	4.0400	4.0604	4.0741	4.0794	4.0808
4.25	4.2951	4.3182	4.3337	4.3397	4.3413
4.50	4.5506	4.5765	4.5939	4.6007	4.6024
4.75	4.8064	4.8352	4.8547	4.8623	4.8642
5.00	5.0625	5.0945	5.1161	5.1245	5.1267
5.25	5.3189	5.3542	5.3781	5.3874	5.3898
5.50	5.5756	5.6144	5.6407	5.6509	5.6536
5.75	5.8326	5.8751	5.9039	5.9151	5.9180
6.00	6.0900	6.1363	6.1677	6.1799	6.1831
6.25	6.3476	6.3980	6.4321	6.4454	6.4488
6.50	6.6056	6.6601	6.6971	6.7115	6.7152
6.75	6.8639	6.9227	6.9627	6.9783	6.9823
7.00	7.1225	7.1859	7.2290	7.2457	7.2500
7.25	7.3814	7.4495	7.4958	7.5138	7.5185
7.50	7.6406	7.7135	7.7632	7.7825	7.7875
7.75	7.9001	7.9781	8.0312	8.0519	8.0573
8.00	8.1600	8.2432	8.2999	8.3220	8.3277
8.25	8.4201	8.5087	8.5692	8.5927	8.5988
8.50	8.6806	8.7747	8.8390	8.8641	8.8706
8.75	8.9414	9.0413	9.1095	9.1362	9.1430
9.00	9.2025	9.3083	9.3806	9.4089	9.4162
9.25	9.4639	9.5758	9.6524	9.6823	9.6900
9.50	9.7256	9.8438	9.9247	9.9563	9.9645
9.75	9.9876	10.1123	10.1977	10.2310	10.2397
10.00	10.2500	10.3812	10.4713	10.5064	10.5155
11.00	11.3025	11.4621	11.5718	11.6148	11.6259

12.00	12.3600	12.5508	12.6825	12.7340	12.7474
13.00	13.4225	13.6475	13.8032	13.8643	13.8802
14.00	14.4900	14.7523	14.9342	15.0057	15.0242
15.00	15.5625	15.8650	16.0754	16.1583	16.1798

Appendix C

	FOR SSA USE ONLY

REQUEST FOR STATEMENT OF EARNINGS
(PLEASE PRINT IN INK OR USE TYPEWRITER)

AX •

SP •

I REQUEST A SUMMARY STATEMENT OF EARNINGS FROM MY SOCIAL SECURITY RECORD

NH Full name you use in work or business

First | Middle Initial | Last
,

SN Social security number shown on your card

Your date of birth

DB | Month | Day | Year | **A**

MA Other Social Security number(s) you have used

Your Sex

SX ☐ Male   ☐ Female

AK Other name(s) you have used (Include your maiden name)

PRIVACY STATEMENT

The Social Security Administration (SSA) is authorized to collect information asked on this form under section 205 of the Social Security Act. It is needed so SSA can quickly identify your record and prepare the earnings statement you requested. While you are not required to furnish the information, failure to do so may prevent your request from being processed. The information will be used primarily for issuing your earnings statement.

I am the individual to whom the record pertains. I understand that if I knowingly and willingly request or receive a record about an individual under false pretenses I would be guilty of a Federal crime and could be fined up to $5000.

Sign your name here: (Do not print) | Date

▶

I AUTHORIZE YOU TO SEND THE STATEMENT TO THE NAME AND ADDRESS BELOW: *(To be completed in all cases)*

PN Name of the addressee

AD Street number and name

City and state | **ZP** | Zip Code

Form **SSA-7004 PC OP 1**   (9-82) Previous Editions are Obsolete

Glossary

accrued interest: The interest due on a bond or other fixed-income security that must be paid by the buyer of the security to the seller.

annuity: A contract where the buyer (annuitant) pays a sum of money to receive regular payments for life or a fixed period of time.

asked price: The net asset value per share plus sales charge, if any. The asked price of a stock refers to the price at which the seller is willing to sell.

asset: Any item of value. Several classifications including these: tangible asset—an item that can readily be assigned a dollar value (hard assets fall into this category, but it is usually reserved for gold and silver); current asset—an item that can be turned into cash in a year or less; fixed asset—an item used for business, such as machinery; intangible asset—an item that cannot be readily assigned a dollar value, like the goodwill of a business.

automatic reinvestment: A plan that allows shareholders to receive dividend distributions in the form of new shares instead of cash.

automatic withdrawal: See check-a-month plan.

back-end load: The fee charged when a redemption takes place. See load.

balance sheet: A financial statement showing the dollar amounts of a company's or person's assets, liabilities, and owner's equity.

balanced fund: A mutual fund which has an investment policy of "balancing" its portfolio, generally by including bonds, preferred stocks, and common stocks.

bankers' acceptances (BAs): Short-term, noninterest-bearing notes sold at a discount and redeemed at maturity for full face value. Primarily used to finance foreign trade. BAs represent a future claim on a U.S. bank that provides lines of credit to U.S. importers. BAs are collateralized by the goods to be sold and are guaranteed by the importer's U.S. bank.

basis point: Term used to describe amount of change in yield. One hundred basis points equal 1%. An increase from 8% to 10% would be a change of 200 basis points.

bear market: A sustained period of falling stock prices usually preceding or accompanied by a period of poor economic performance known as a recession. The opposite of a bull market.

beta: Term used to describe the price volatility of securities. Standard and Poor's Index is set at a beta of one; anything assigned a beta above one is considered to be more volatile than the Index; anything below one has less volatility than the S&P Index.

bid: The price at which someone will buy a security.

blue chip: The common stock of a major corporation with a long, relatively stable record of earnings and dividend payments.

bond: A security representing debt; a loan from the bondholder to the corporation. The bondholder usually receives semiannual interest payments with principal being refunded at maturity.

bond fund: A mutual fund whose portfolio consists primarily of bonds. The emphasis is normally on income rather than growth.

bond maturity: The time at which an issuer redeems a bond. The investor is paid the full face value plus any accrued interest.

broker: A person in the business of effecting securities transactions for others, for a commission. There are two types of brokers: full service brokers who give advice and discount brokers, who do not give advice (the investor must do his own research).

bull market: A stock market that is characterized by rising prices over a long period of time. The time span is not precise, but it represents a period of investor optimism, lower interest rates, and economic growth. The opposite of a bear market.

capital appreciation: An increase in value, such as in real estate, stock or bond prices.

capital gain: A long-term capital gain is a profit from the sale of a capital asset, such as a security, that has been held for over six months. A short-term capital gain is the profit from selling a capital asset in less than six months. Both are subject to federal tax at ordinary income rates.

capital loss: A loss from the sale of a capital asset. Up to $3,000 may be deducted in one year, and if the loss is greater than the amount allowed for one year, the excess may be carried over to future years until it is used up.

cash flow: The cash flow from an investment is the total of dividends, interest payments, realized profits, and any return of principal you receive.

cash value: Certain types of life insurance policies allow a "savings portion" of the premium payment to accumulate to a cash value.

certificate: The actual piece of paper which certifies ownership of stock in a corporation.

certificate of deposit (CD): Generally, a short-term debt instrument certificate issued by commercial banks or savings and loan associations. (Euro CDs are issued by foreign branches of U.S. banks; Yankee CDs are issued by U.S. branches of foreign banks.)

check-a-month plan: An arrangement many open-end companies have which enables investors to receive fixed payments, usually monthly or quarterly. The actual payout is determined by the investor.

closed-end management company: A company that issues a fixed number of shares that usually must be traded in the securities market. Closed-end investment company shares are usually bought and sold through brokers.

COLA: Cost-of-living adjustment.

collectible: A physical object which has value by virtue of its rarity, intrinsic or artistic value.

commercial paper (CP): Unsecured promissory notes of corporations, with maturities of up to 270 days. Used as a money market instrument.

commission: The fee paid to a broker for buying or selling securities as an agent.

common-law employee: An employee who works for a self-employed person, a partnership, or a corporation but who has no financial interest in the employer's trade, business, or profession.

common stock: Securities that represent ownership in a corporation.

compound interest: Interest computed on the interest as well as the principal.

consumer price index (CPI): Index that analyzes the change in prices for consumer goods and services over time.

conversion privilege: See exchange privilege.

convertible securities: A bond, debenture or preferred stock that gives its owner the right to exchange that security for common stock or another type of security issued by the same company.

correction: Used in conjunction with a bull market. It is a sustained period of stock price declining in the midst of long-term rising stock prices. Corrections are usually followed by another period of rising stock prices. A major correction refers to a decline of 10% or more in the widely accepted stock market indexes.

coupon: A promise to pay interest when due, coupons are usually attached to a bond. When the coupon comes due, it is clipped and presented for payment. The term also refers to a bond's stated interest rate.

custodian: The organization which holds in custody and safekeeping the securities and other assets of a mutual fund or individual.

DEFRA: Deficit Reduction Act of 1984.

dealer: A person or firm who regularly buys and sells securities for others from his or her own account of securities. In contrast, a broker acts as an agent for others. Frequently, broker and dealer functions are synonymous.

debenture: A bond secured by the general credit of the corporation, and usually not secured by any collateral.

debt instrument: Any instrument that signifies a loan between a borrower and a lender.

declaration of dividends: Announcement by issuer of bonds or equities of their decision to make a payment to their shareholders. Some companies do this on a regular basis, while others may declare a dividend only when company earnings have reached a certain predetermined level. Many money funds declare dividends daily but pay monthly.

deep discount bond: A type of bond that is selling below 80% of its par (face) value. The face value of a bond is usually $1,000.

defined benefit plan: A retirement plan offered by employers that promises to pay out a predetermined annual amount during retirement years.

depreciation: The estimated decline in the value of property due to use, deterioration, or obsolescence over a period of time.

discretionary accounts: An account in which an investment adviser or broker has the full right to buy and sell securities without consultation or authorization of the investor.

discount: The amount by which a preferred stock or bond may sell below its face value.

distributions: Dividends paid from net investment income and payments made from realized capital gains of a mutual fund.

distributor: The principal underwriter—either a person or a company—that purchases open-end investment company shares directly from the issuer for resale to others.

distribution fee: Under 12b-1 plans, a fund that does not have its own sales force is allowed to take a percentage of the assets as a fee to pay independent brokers for selling its funds.

diversification: The policy of spreading investments among a number of different securities to reduce the risk inherent in investing. Diversification may be among types of securities, different companies, different industries, or different geographical locations.

diversified investment company: To be so classified, the Investment Company Act requires that 75% of a fund's assets be allocated so that not more than 5% of its total assets are invested in one company. In addition, it can hold no more than 10% of the outstanding voting securities of another company.

dividend: A payment declared by a corporation's board of directors, and made to shareholders, usually on a quarterly basis.

dollar cost-averaging: Method of investing equal amounts of money at regular intervals regardless of whether the stock market is moving upward or downward. The theory is that the investor's average cost will be lower than if he invested larger amounts irregularly over the same amount of time.

earned income: Net profits derived from the business, less retirement plan contributions, for a self-employed person. For "common-law" employees of a self-employed or corporate business, earnings are taxable wages received.

employee stock ownership plan (ESOP): A qualified employee benefit plan which invests in securities of the parent company.

equity: Represents stock ownership of a company.

equity fund: A mutual fund that invests primarily in stocks.

ERISA: The Employee Retirement Income Security Act of 1974. It represented the most sweeping overhaul of pension and employee benefit rules in four decades. ERISA requires that if an employer elects to provide employee benefits, the benefits must meet ERISA guidelines under labor and tax law provisions. ERISA rules have since been overhauled by legislation enacted in 1982 and 1984.

Eurodollars: U.S. dollars deposited in foreign branches of U.S. banks or foreign banks located outside the U.S.

exchange privilege: The right to take all or some of the shares of one fund and put them into another fund within the same family of funds. This is considered a sale and new purchase for tax purposes. (Same as a conversion or switching privilege.)

ex-dividend date: The date on which stock is sold without dividend. Under the five-day delivery plan, buyers of the stock on the fourth business day preceding the stockholder of record date will not receive the declared dividend. Most stock exchanges operate on the five-day plan.

face value: The value that appears on the face of a bond. This is the amount the issuing company will pay at maturity, but it does not necessarily indicate market price.

family of funds: A group of mutual funds managed by the same investment company. One company may manage several different funds, each with different objectives, such as growth, income, or tax-exempt funds.

FDIC (Federal Deposit Insurance Corporation): The federal agency which insures deposits up to $100,000 at member banks. FDIC also makes loans to buy assets from member banks to facilitate mergers or help prevent bank failures.

fiduciary: An individual or corporation who is entrusted with certain assets for a specified purpose. Also known as trustee, executor, guardian.

fixed annuity: An annuity contract that provides for fixed payments at regular intervals.

401(k): A qualified employee benefit plan where employee contributions are made on a pretax basis. Both employer and employee contributions compound tax free until withdrawn.

front-end load: A sales charge for buying into a mutual fund.

frozen plan: A qualified retirement plan to which contributions are no longer being made.

FSLIC (Federal Savings and Loan Insurance Corporation): The federal agency established to insure funds on deposit at member S&Ls.

fully invested: One hundred percent invested position..All money is considered to be earning dividends, capital gains, interest, or a mixture of any of these, in contrast to only a portion of the invested money having earning capabilities.

fund assets: The total dollar amount invested in a fund.

fund representative: A federally licensed (registered) person qualified to give investors information about, and sell, a fund.

government securities: A general term that includes any instruments of debt issued by the U.S. government.

gross income: Income before any deductions or expenses are taken out.

growth fund: A mutual fund which has growth of capital as its primary objective, to be obtained principally through investments in common stocks with growth potential. This type of fund will primarily generate long- and short-term capital gains rather than pay dividends.

growth-income fund: A mutual fund whose objective is to provide both income and long-term growth.

guaranteed investment contract (GIC): A fixed income investment with a specified interest rate and date of maturity. Offered by insurance companies, it is a common investment vehicle selected for voluntary contribution funds.

holding company: A company that owns the majority of stock or securities of, as well as manages, one or more other companies.

illiquid: An asset that is difficult to convert into cash quickly.

immediate annuity: An annuity contract that starts making payments to the annuitant almost immediately—within one year of the contract's purchase.

income fund: A mutual fund which has current income as its primary objective.

index: A mathematically derived number used as an indicator of trends in the market.

Individual Retirement Account: A retirement plan that can be started by anyone who earns employment income. Investment earnings on IRA money are tax-deferred, usually until retirement at age 59½ or older. The deductibility of annual IRA contributions is limited to taxpayers who meet income guidelines defined in the Tax Code of 1986.

inflation: The economic condition of rising prices for goods and services. It is characterized by an increasing volume of currency in circulation and a decline in the buying power of cash.

institutions-only funds: Funds that allow only corporate, depository institution or pension fund investors to buy shares. Some funds which claim to be institutions-only will allow individuals to invest if they can meet the (usually high) minimum initial investment.

interest: Periodic payments made to a lender of money by the borrower for use of the money borrowed.

investment company: Generic term including mutual funds, unit investment trusts, and other types of companies that sell their shares to the public and invest the proceeds according to stated investment objectives.

investment objective: The specific goal, such as long-term capital growth or current income, which the investor or mutual fund pursues.

IRA: See Individual Retirement Account.

IRA rollover: The removal of IRA money from one investment and placement of this money into another investment. A rollover involves the individual receiving the money and reinvesting it. Rollovers must be completed within 60 days and are only allowed once a year.

IRA transfer: Movement of IRA funds from one investment to another. The IRA investor does not receive the money; it goes directly into the other investment. A transfer is allowed at any time.

Keogh plan: A tax-qualified retirement program for self-employed individuals and their employees.

leverage: The use of borrowed money with invested funds to increase returns. The effect is to magnify profits or losses and increase the amount of risk. (See margin.)

liability: Any debt owed by a company or individual. Usually classified as a current liability (due in one year or less) or a long-term liability (due in over one year).

liquid: May be easily converted into cash or exchanged for other assets.

liquidate: To convert an asset into cash.

load: A portion of the offering price that goes toward selling costs such as sales commissions and distribution. A front-end load is the fee charged when buying into a fund. A back-end load is the fee charged when getting out of a fund.

long-term investment: For federal tax purposes, an investment held for over six months.

lump sum distribution: A payment made to an individual of the proceeds of his or her employee benefit plan account.

management company: A company that manages the day-to-day operations of a mutual fund. See open-end and closed-end management company. (Also called an investment company.)

management fee: The amount paid to the administrator and/or management company (who may also serve as an investment adviser) for service.

margin account: A brokerage account that allows an investor to buy or sell securities on credit. An investor can purchase additional securities against the value of cash and securities in the account.

margin, buying on: Buying securities on credit from a broker.

market order: An order to buy or sell a stated amount of a security at the best possible price as soon as it can be accomplished.

market price: The last reported price at which a security has been sold.

market rate: A general term used to describe the current interest rate on a given instrument.

maturity: The scheduled date for repayment of the principal amount of a debt instrument.

money market fund: Mutual fund which invests in short-term, relatively riskless money market instruments such as bank certificates of deposit, bankers' acceptances, commercial paper, and short-term government securities.

municipal bond fund: An open-end company or unit investment trust which invests in diversified holdings of federal tax-exempt securities issued by state, city, and local governments.

mutual fund: An open-end or closed-end investment company which pools the money of its shareholders into one professionally managed account; investments are made in a wide variety of securities.

net asset value per share: The total market value of an investment company's shares—securities, cash, and any accrued earnings—minus its liabilities, and then divided by the number of shares outstanding.

net income: Income less expenses and deductions.

no-load fund: A fund which does not charge sales fees. Investors purchase shares directly from the fund, rather than through an investment dealer or broker.

NOW account: Negotiable order of withdrawal account. An interest-bearing checking and savings account.

odd lot: The usual amount when buying shares of stock is 100 shares (a "round lot"). When you buy less than 100 shares it is called an odd lot; commissions vary with the number of shares bought.

offering price: The lowest price at which shares are offered for sale. (Also called asked price.)

open-end management company: An investment company that continuously sells and redeems shares.

option: The right to buy (call option) or sell (put option) a fixed quantity of a security, at a stated price, within a specific amount of time.

options fund: A mutual fund which sells options on its shares to increase its income.

ordinary income: Income taxed at the maximum rate schedule, such as employment income or income from a business.

over-the-counter: The nationwide network of brokers/dealers who buy and sell securities that, for the most part, are not listed on an exchange.

owner-employee: A self-employed person who owns or who has at least a 10% interest in a business or partnership.

penny stock: Any stock that is very low-priced and often speculative.

periodic payment plan: An arrangement which allows an investor to purchase mutual fund shares periodically, usually with provisions for the reinvestment of income dividends and the acceptance of capital gains distributions in additional shares.

plan administrator: The individual who maintains records, prepares reports, and generally manages a group's employee benefit plan.

portfolio: The total investment holdings owned by an investment company or an individual.

preferred stock: A class of stock that has prior claim on dividends before common stockholders. In the event of corporate liquidation, preferred stockholders have a prior claim on assets over common shareholders.

premium: The amount by which a bond or preferred stock sells above its face value.

profit: The amount earned when the selling price is higher than the cost.

prospectus: The official written statement which describes a mutual fund, or any security, and offers it for sale. In the case of a fund, the prospectus contains information required by the Securities and Exchange Commission on investment objectives and policies, services, investment restrictions, officers and directors, procedure to buy and sell shares, fees, and financial statements.

proxy: The written transfer of voting rights to someone who will then vote according to the wishes of the shareholder. Usually done if the shareholder cannot be present at the stockholders' meeting.

qualified retirement plan: A private retirement plan that meets the rules and regulations of the Internal Revenue Service. Earnings on contributions made to such plans are tax-deferred, usually until retirement. Most company pension plans are qualified retirement plans.

redeem: To buy back shares from the present owner. See redemption price.

redemption price: The amount per share a mutual fund shareholder receives when he cashes in his shares (also known as "liquidating price" or "bid price"). The value of the shares depends on the market value of the company's portfolio securities at the time.

reinvestment privilege: A service provided by most mutual funds for the automatic purchase of additional shares with the shareholder's dividends and capital gains distributions.

return on investment: Percent gain including reinvestment of capital gains and dividends, if any.

rollover: Reinvestment of funds into a similar investment. With retirement plans, a rollover occurs when assets from one type of qualified plan are moved to another.

round lot: The accepted standard number of shares (100) used to trade stocks. It is also the number of shares to which prevailing broker commission rates apply.

sales charge: The amount charged in connection with public distribution of fund shares. It is added to the net asset value per share in computing the offering price and is paid to the dealer and underwriter.

Securities and Exchange Commission (SEC): An independent agency of the U.S. government which administers the various federal securities laws for the protection of the shareholder.

SEP (Simplified Employee Pension): A qualified employee retirement plan where the employer makes contributions to the employees' IRAs.

series funds: A broad range of funds offered by a fund family. Each fund has its own investment philosophy whereby it invests in only certain industries or companies.

signature guarantee: A required signature by a fiduciary representative (banker or broker) to verify the identity of the shareholder.

short-term investment: An investment of less than one year. For tax purposes, short-term is now considered less than six months.

social security integration: A method of coordinating employer Social Security and retirement plan contributions.

special purpose fund: A fund that has certain requirements that must be met by prospective investors before they may invest.

specialized mutual fund: A fund that focuses on a particular segment of the market and has a philosophy or stipulation the fund must follow or meet when investing.

speculative: Considered to have a high degree of risk.

split: A division of a company's shares into a greater or lesser number. Often a split is designed to lower the cost of a share, making it more attractive. A stock split does not affect a shareholder's proportional interest in the company.

stock dividend: A dividend paid in securities rather than cash.

switch: See exchange privilege.

tax avoidance: Legal actions that may be taken to reduce or eliminate tax liabilities.

tax-deferred: Income on which a tax is levied only when it is distributed.

tax-exempt securities: Usually refers to municipal bonds that are exempt from federal taxes. Some municipal bonds, known as triple exempt bonds, are also exempt from state and local taxes depending on the state laws where the bond was issued and where the buyer of the bond resides.

tax-exempt fund (tax-free fund): A mutual fund whose portfolio consists of securities (usually municipal bonds) exempt from federal income tax.

tax shelter: An investment used for deferring taxes.

TEFRA: The Tax Equity and Fiscal Responsibility Act of 1982.

total return: Dividend plus change in price on an investment.

Treasury bill (T-bill): Short-term debt issued by the U.S. government at a discount from its face value. Maturities are three months, six months, and one year. Minimum order is $10,000 with subsequent multiples of $5,000.

Treasury bond: Debt obligation issued by the U.S. government with a maturity ranging from ten to thirty years and with $1,000 as the lowest denomination.

Treasury note: Debt obligation issued by the U.S. government with a maturity between one year and ten years. Lowest denomination issued is $1,000.

trustee: The institution that maintains administrative control over another's assets: a commercial bank, savings and loan association, mutual savings bank, trust company, or stockbroker.

Truth-in-Lending Law: A federal law stating lenders must specify the terms and conditions of the loan to the borrower.

unit investment trust (UIT): A type of mutual fund that buys a fixed number of debt obligations and sells them to investors in units. Most common types of obligations are federal agency obligations, municipal bonds and utility obligations.

variable annuity: An insurance annuity contract under which the dollar payments received are not fixed but fluctuate with the market. Most frequently, investors will have a choice of stock, money, or bond funds.

vesting: An employee benefit plan participant's rights of ownership to the employer contributions made on his or her behalf, plus earnings on those contributions.

withdrawal plan: A mutual fund plan that allows a specified amount of money to be withdrawn at specified intervals.

wire transfer: Use of a bank to send money to a fund or vice versa.

yield: Income earned from investments, usually expressed as a percentage of market price; also referred to as return.

zero-coupon bond: A bond sold at a deep discount on which no periodic interest payments are made prior to maturity. Payment of principal at maturity provides an effective yield on the amount for which it was purchased.

Index

ABOUT THE AUTHOR

"America's do-it-yourself investment guru," William E. Donoghue is not only the author of three personal finance bestsellers but is also chairman of The Donoghue Organization, Inc. (TDO), which is based in Holliston, Massachusetts, about 35 miles southwest of Boston. TDO and its staff of more than 40 professionals are dedicated to providing independent analyses of trends in the financial services industry for consumers, regulators, and corporations.

Donoghue, however, has always had a special affinity for the independent investor and has taught his do-it-yourself investment philosophy to thousands by providing easy-to-understand investment strategies through his newsletter, *Donoghue's MONEYLETTER*.

Published twice each month, *Donoghue's MONEYLETTER* provides the reader with a bird's-eye view of trends and developments in the financial markets in language that even a novice can understand. Yet the basic investment strategies outlined in *Donoghue's MONEYLETTER* have outperformed the majority of all mutual funds in existence for the past five years while minimizing risk.

Donoghue is so proud of his newsletter, which was named "Best Financial Advisory Newletter" by the Newsletter Association in 1986, that he would like to send you a *free* sample copy of *Donoghue's MONEYLETTER* for your review. You also get your choice of one of his special reports, *New Tax Strategies* or *Today's Best and Most Dangerous Investment Deals.* Please use the form below for ordering your *free* sample copy of *Donoghue's MONEYLETTER* and your choice of a *free* special report. Mail it to The Donoghue Organization, 360 Woodland St., P.O. Box 540, Holliston, MA 01746.

- -

FREE! To readers of *Donoghue's Investment Tips for Retirement Savings,* a sample copy of *Donoghue's MONEYLETTER* and your choice of a special report. Please make your choice below of either *New Tax Strategies* or *Today's Best and Most Dangerous Investment Deals* and mail this coupon now!

Your choice of special reports (please check one):

☐ *New Tax Strategies*   ☐ *Today's Best and Most Dangerous Investment Deals*

NAME _____

STREET ADDRESS _____

CITY, STATE & ZIP _____